A Short History of British Columbia

Dr. Ed Whitcomb

From Sea to Sea Enterprises
Ottawa

Library and Archives Canada Cataloguing in Publication

Whitcomb, Dr. Edward A.
A Short History of British Columbia / Ed Whitcomb.

Includes index.
ISBN 0-9694667-4-9

1. British Columbia – History. I. Title.

FC3811.W44 2006 971.1
C2006-903595-4

© From Sea To Sea Enterprises, 2006
2130 Dutton Crescent, Ottawa,
Ontario, Canada, K1J 6K4
www.fromseatosea.com

Printed in Canada by Dollco Printing, Ottawa

TABLE OF CONTENTS

Preface...v

Map of Railways 34

1. The British Columbia of the Native Peoples, to 1810.................... 1

2. New Caledonia, 1810-1855... 6

3. Confederation, 1855-1871...10

4. Broken Promises and Threats of Secession, 1871-1885.................17

5. Unsteady Progress, 1885-1900...22

6. The Great Boom, 1900-1914...29

7. The Great War and the Troubled Twenties, 1914-1929.................36

8. The Great Depression, 1930-1939..42

9. World War II and the Post-War Boom, 1945-1952.....................48

10. Social Credit, 1952-1972...53

11. New Democrats and New Social Creditors, 1972-1985.................60

    Suggestions for Further Reading...66

    Index...67

*This Book is Dedicated to the
people of British Columbia*

Preface

This is the fourth in a series of history books on Canada's ten provinces. The idea for this series first arose in 1969 when I moved to Nova Scotia. Being new to the province and knowing very little about it, I went looking for a short history book which would provide an outline of the development of my newly-adopted home. There was no such book. In fact, there were hardly any short histories of Canada's provinces. In 1975 I decided to write the sort of book I had been looking for, and started with my native province of Manitoba. Over 7,000 copies of that Short History of Manitoba have been sold, which suggests that I was not alone in wanting good, short provincial histories. The project to write histories of all the provinces was delayed by family and career, but the Centennials of Alberta and Saskatchewan put the series back on track, and the short histories of those provinces were published in 2005.

This Short History of British Columbia is designed to provide the average reader with a quick but accurate survey of the broad outline of British Columbia's development. The emphasis in this book is on the political developments that shaped the province as it is today, subjects such as the Natives, immigration and settlement, economic activities like the fur trade, fishing and mining, and the attainment of provincial status. It explains the reasons for the boom that preceded the First World War and the depression that followed, including such issues as prohibition and women's suffrage. The Depression, Social Credit, resource development, and more modern developments complete the account.

Every historian has a point of view that determines which of the thousands of issues he or she will discuss, which of the millions of facts he or she will relate, and what things he or she will emphasize or ignore. This is essentially a political history, with some reference to economic and social developments, and it clearly emphasizes provincial rather than national or local developments. It seeks to explain British Columbia's side in disputes between the province and the federal government. It is not "popular history", and does not include pictures because there are several excellent picture books of BC identified in the section Suggested Reading. While the achievements of British Columbians are documented, some criticisms are made of the heroes, politicians and groups who have shaped the province. In short, it is but one perspective on a very fascinating and complex society. My greatest hope is that this small book will encourage others to read more and to write more on the dozens of issues and perspectives necessary to obtain a full understanding of any society's development.

This account ends with the mid-1980s. Several readers thought it should cover more recent developments, but there is a point where history merges into political science or journalism. While we know the broad outline of recent events, we do not have access to Cabinet decisions, correspondence or the memoirs of most participants. Many issues are still current, some still the subject of sharp debate, and many views on them are more subjective than objective. Much research has to be done and many books and articles written before the recent past falls into a proper historical perspective. Perhaps a revised edition in 2025 will bring the story up to 2006!

Many people helped with the preparation of this book. A number of professors, editors, analysts and experts read the full text and made many valuable corrections and suggestions. They include Dr. Jean Barman, Dr. Ted Binnema Dr. R. Matthew Bray, Dr. Keith Christie, Chris Cooter, Dr. Gerald Friesen, Alex Inglis, Dr. Dan Livermore, Dr. Robert McDonald, and Dr. Patricia Roy. I alone am responsible for the weaknesses that remain in the book. The cover designs and maps were done by Linda Turenne, and the colours are those of the official BC flag. Chomchon Tummanon did the formatting and page layouts. John Colyer of Dellco Printers helped with the technical details. Most helpful of all were my wife, Kai, and daughters Denise and Diana whose support and patience made the book possible.

Ottawa, June, 2006.

Chapter One
The British Columbia of the Native Peoples, to 1810

British Columbia was discovered, explored and settled by Aboriginal or Native people. They came from Asia over12,000 years ago, crossing the Bering Strait from Siberia in northeast Asia. Each wave of migration pushed the previous ones farther south and east, possibly down a passageway east of the Rockies that had opened up between the huge ice fields that once covered the land. The Natives of British Columbia (BC) came from north and east of the Rockies or from the north along the coast as the valleys between the mountains emerged from the ice fields, though one theory suggests that they came from across the Pacific.

The area they entered was dominated by mountain ranges. The westerly mountains form Vancouver Island and the Queen Charlotte Islands. On the mainland a series of rugged mountain ranges runs north-west to south-east, including the Coastal, Skeena, Monashee, Selkirk and Purcell ranges. They climax in the mighty Rockies which divide North America, waters to the west flowing into the Pacific, waters to the east flowing into the Arctic or the Gulf of Mexico.

Two major areas are less mountainous. One is the interior plateau where the Fraser, Columbia and Peace Rivers originate. The other is the northeast corner of the province, which is an extension of the prairie and tundra of northern Alberta and the southern Yukon. This mountainous landscape made BC one of the most difficult areas in North America to explore, travel through or develop economically, and has defined the character, history and attitudes of its inhabitants.

One of the outstanding characteristics of BC is its sheer size. It is 800 kilometers or 500 miles from east to west, 1,300 kilometers or 800 miles from north to south, a total of 950,000 square kilometers or 360,000 square miles, making it Canada's third largest province. Forty-five percent of BC is mountain or desert, less than five percent is suitable for agriculture, and half the province is covered in forest. Along the coast, abundant rainfall and mild climate produce giant stands of cedar, Douglas fir, hemlock and alder. In the drier and colder interior, birch, poplar, pine and spruce dominate along with grasslands.

Geographically, BC can be divided into ten regions. Vancouver Island is characterized by a rugged Pacific coast and the less mountainous eastern lowlands. Directly across the Strait of Georgia is the Lower Mainland, centered on the Fraser River delta which runs about 150 kilometers from Vancouver to Hope. Its size, flatness, rich agricultural land and harbours have made it the centre of population, accounting for around 70% of the province's residents today. Running northeast from Hope is the southern interior, centering on the Fraser River Canyon and extending into the areas known as the Cariboo and Chilcotin with population centres like Lytton and Lillooet. It is the main transportation corridor of the province, with an economy also based on ranching.

The Okanagan, surrounding the lake that gives it the name, lies along the American border (49 degrees latitude) and east of the Lower Mainland. A superb dry and mild climate favours fruit-growing, tourism and retirement living. Directly east lie the West and East Kootenays, regions characterized by rugged mountain ranges and rivers running north to south. Its economy was based on some of the richest mineral deposits in the world.

North of Vancouver are the central coast region, between the Fraser and Bella Coola Rivers, and the northwest region, covering almost one fifth of the province and running up to the northern border with the Yukon at 60 degrees latitude. For historical reasons, the Pacific coast north of 54' 40" is part of Alaska. These regions are so rugged that habitation is limited to a few isolated settlements, the economy based mainly on fishing and forestry and the port city of Prince Rupert.

The northeast comprises another fifth of the province, bounded on the north by the Yukon and on the east by Alberta at 120 degrees longitude. This region lies to the east of the Rockies and is drained by the Peace River which flows to the Arctic. The southern part contains good agricultural land and oil and gas reserves. Between the northeast and the southern interior lies the central interior centered on Prince George and the upper Fraser Valley, a region of more gentle mountains and valleys.

Because of the mountainous terrain and perhaps because they have lived longer in BC than elsewhere, Native settlement, society, language patterns and organization were quite different from those in the rest of Canada. There the Natives were organized in large nations, and the Cree language was spoken from the Rockies to Quebec. But in BC the mountainous terrain divided the Natives into seven linguistic and cultural groups. They correspond to some degree to the geographic regions of the province. The Haida lived in the Queen Charlotte Islands, the Kwakiutl on Northern Vancouver Island, and the Nootka on the rest of Vancouver Island and in the Lower Mainland. The Salish occupied the Fraser delta, plus some pockets along the coast on the Fraser and Bella Coola Rivers.

In the southeast corner of the province, the valleys of the Columbia and Thompson Rivers were occupied by the Kootenays, and Athapaskan peoples lived in the northeast. The Prince Rupert area was home to the Tsimshian, and the northwest to the Tlingit. These seven broad linguistic groups contained perhaps three dozen dialects, some of which are identified with bands like the Slave and Beaver in the northeast or the Chilcotin in the central interior. Overall, there were perhaps 200-300 smaller distinct bands, sometimes occupying just one valley, with distinct languages which might have little similarity to the language spoken in the next valley. But despite the mountains there were numerous contacts between bands, much commonality of customs, and some trade.

Estimates for the number of Natives at the time of first contact with white explorers vary from 80,000 to 250,000. Culturally, Natives could be divided into two broad groups. Along the coast, salmon provided an abundant and guaranteed supply of food, which could be harvested easily and regularly due to the annual spawning runs up the rivers. As a result, coastal Natives developed permanent settlements with fairly sophisticated societies. The Nootka, for example, hunted whales in canoes carved from thirty-foot lengths of cedar, and the Salish wove blankets from the wool of a now-extinct dog.

The coastal bands lived in huge cedar houses, some big enough to accommodate thirty families. Their societies had a strict hierarchy, with hereditary royalty, nobles, commoners and slaves, the latter coming from raids on neighbouring bands. Rank carried responsibility for leadership and the well-being of the community, with matching privilege, such as access to better fishing sites. Huge totem poles provided a visual and religious symbol to the coastal villages.

In the interior, the Natives had to migrate continuously because their food supply was often inadequate. The interior Natives lived in small bands, making only those objects they could move from camp to camp. Their societies shared some aspects of those on the coast, but lacked the wealth and elaborate political, social or cultural development of the coastal tribes. Generally the men hunted, fished and carved religious symbols like face masks. Women tanned hides, made clothing, preserved food, transported goods, and raised the children.

Native chiefs were obliged to share their wealth, an act which demonstrated their position and status. This was done through massive celebrations called potlatchs, which would coincide with visits, births or funerals, or simply some need to demonstrate status. Gifts and possessions accumulated over the years would be bestowed on members of the clan and on guests, the quality and quantity establishing the donor's wealth and authority. Such gifts might then be passed on in a subsequent potlatch. Interior natives had similar but far less lavish practices.

Native society placed considerable emphasis on an individual's obligations to the community. Their gods had provided land and water and resources for all the people. Those who could hunt and fish did so, acquiring what was needed, and sharing with everyone. Religion acknowledged creation and a debt to the creator, and emphasized the concept of harmony between man and nature and within each group. Men called shamans filled both religious and medical roles, administering to the ill with a combination of herbal remedies and spirit worship. Concepts of acceptable and unaccept-able behaviour were highly developed and usually followed. Concepts of ownership were flexible – if something was there, it could be used but not destroyed.

Its remote location isolated BC for more than three centuries after the first whites landed in North America. But by the mid-eighteenth century, three different groups were approaching the region: the Russians from the north, the Spanish from the south, and the English from across the Pacific. None knew what was there but all were determined to prevent the others from gaining any advantage. By the 1790s they were joined by Americans coming around Cape Horn and by British explorers coming overland from Montreal.

The Russians were the first. Their rulers had a claim to Alaska, and in 1729 and 1741 sent the Danish sailor Vitrus Bering to explore the coast. It is not clear whether Bering or his crew got as far south as present-day BC, but they did begin the fur trade along the northwest coast. In 1774 Spain enforced its claim over the whole coast north of Mexico by sending Juan Josef Perez Hernandez. He sighted the Queen Charlotte Islands and traded with the Natives. In 1775 another Spanish explorer, Juan Francisco Quadra, visited Vancouver Island. In 1776 the British Government sent Captain James Cook, who explored the islands and coast as far north as Alaska and spent a month at Nootka Sound in the Queen Charlotte Islands.

Captain Cook found the Natives to be skilled and demanding traders. His crew took sea otter pelts to China where demand was enormous and profits extraordinary. Within 20 years the coast was fully explored and mapped. Much of that was done by Quadra and by the British explorer, Captain George Vancouver, who concluded that there was no viable Northwest Passage connecting the Pacific and Atlantic Oceans. These explorers and traders hardly ventured inland, mainly because the coastal Natives immediately became middlemen, making a profit off the trade from farther inland.

Increased competition and the desire to assert sovereignty led both the Spanish and English to establish bases and seize each other's ships and goods. This rivalry almost led to war, but by the Nootka Conventions of 1790 Spain and England agreed to share the trade. Captains Vancouver and Quadra were sent out to administer the Conventions. While they became good friends and explored the coastline together, they could not agree on the terms of the treaty. American sailors were also active. Captain Robert Gray explored the mouth of a huge river which he named the Columbia after his ship. In the 1790s hundreds of ships from Russia, Spain, England and the United States were trading for sea otter pelts up and down the coast. But excessive greed and competition decimated the sea otter population and flooded the Chinese market, and the coastal fur trade soon went into decline.

Almost all of mainland BC was explored by English and Scottish fur traders working for the North West Company (NWC) based in Montreal or the Hudson's Bay Company (HBC) based in London. By the 1780s these explorers were pushing into the Rocky Mountains. In the autumn of 1792 Alexander Mackenzie of the NWC went up the Peace River, up its tributary the Parsnip, and over the Rocky Mountain divide to the headwaters of the Fraser where he spent the winter. The Natives told him it was too dangerous to go down the Fraser, so he portaged northwards to the West Road River, over to the Bella Coola and down to the Pacific by July 21, 1793. He was the first white explorer to cross North America north of Mexico.

This route was too difficult for the fur trade, and little more exploration was done until 1805 when Simon Fraser resumed the task. He established Fort McLeod on a tributary of the Peace River, the oldest permanent white settlement in BC, plus a series of small trading forts. He named the land New Caledonia after his native Scotland. In 1808 his party worked its way around the many rapids on the Fraser and paddled down to its mouth, but confirmed that this route was also too difficult for the fur trade. The greatest of the western explorers and map makers, David Thompson, then took up the challenge. In 1807 he went up the North Saskatchewan and over Howse Pass to the upper Columbia basin. The next year he went down the Kootenay River, and reached the mouth of the Columbia in 1811, two weeks after Americans had established Fort Astoria on its south bank. Thompson later explored the river which Fraser named after him, and Thompson returned the compliment, naming the Fraser River after its main explorer. By the 1820s the overall outline of the future province and its rivers, lakes and mountain ranges were well understood by European and Canadian explorers.

Chapter Two
New Caledonia, 1810-1855

For a century after contact with the whites, economic activity and everyday life remained much the same as they had for centuries. The Native economy continued to be based on fishing and hunting. They built their homes out of cedar and other wood, making their clothing, instruments and religious objects out of wood, stone, furs and feathers, and trading with neighbouring Native bands.

At first the fur trade with the whites did not significantly alter their customary way of life. Blankets of wool and pots of iron were vastly superior to what they had manufactured out of wood and stone, so they willingly traded furs for these better products. The Natives had traded with their neighbours for centuries, sometimes turning meetings into social events, and they were shrewd judges of quality and value. They quickly learned the value of the white man's goods in terms of their own wants and needs, the value of furs to the white traders, the advantage of playing Russians, English and Americans against each other, and even the advantage of delaying trade as the whites were always impatient to leave.

Coastal Natives immediately established themselves as middlemen, taking a profit on the trade with the Natives of the interior. They used their increased wealth to carry their traditional culture to new heights, as demonstrated by more ostentatious potlatches and an explosion in the production of totem poles and wood carvings. Natives became partners in the fur trade, providing guides, couriers, transportation, food, and a growing labour force around the forts. Native women married white fur traders, which enhanced the status of the women and cemented alliances between chiefs, tribes and fur traders. A mixed population of Metis grew up around the forts, people at ease in white or Native society. James Douglas, the HBC Chief Factor in the mid-1800s, had a Native wife, and his daughters married prominent members of the fledgling white society.

The main effect of contact with the whites was the impact of European diseases from which the Natives had no immunity. In the first century of contact smallpox, tuberculosis, influenza, venereal disease, measles and alcoholism drastically reduced the population. As trade grew, violence also increased. There was sporadic violence between traders and Natives over misunderstandings, cheating, and theft. The same factors produced increasing violence between Natives of different bands, worsened by the acquisition of better weapons. The HBC was quick and forceful but generally fair in dealing with violence. But Natives received harsher treatment and less attention to their complaints than did whites.

By 1810 the NWC had established a string of forts in the interior. The furs were sent upriver to the Rockies and then over the main prairie transportation routes that took them thousands of miles to Montreal. American traders were also active in the area, a rough division giving the NWC the area north and west of the Columbia, the Americans dominating south and east of the Columbia and trading north into the Okanagan and the Kootenays. East of the Rockies the HBC and NWC were locked in a bitter battle for dominance. That rivalry ended in 1821 with the amalgamation of the two companies under the HBC. It then rationalized the trading system, re-organizing the routes, lowering costs, ending the use of liquor, and effectively governing the region for four decades. In 1824 HBC Governor George Simpson made an inspection tour of the region. His recommendations led to more efficiency, faster trade routes and the growing of food near the forts to reduce costs.

To offset American forts on the south bank of the Columbia, the HBC built Fort Vancouver in 1824 on the north bank, 120 kilometers from the mouth of the river. An agreement in 1819 established the 49th parallel as the border between the United States and British North America east of the Rockies, with the fur trade of the Columbia River basin open to both sides. Competition with the Americans on the northwest coast ended when the HBC obtained a monopoly to supply the Russian forts in Alaska. In 1821 Britain recognized Russian sovereignty over that coast as far south as 54' 40", which remains the coastal boundary between BC and Alaska.

In 1842 the 39-year old James Douglas was appointed Chief Factor of the HBC west of the Rockies, in effect, the governor of the whole vast land. A man of mixed Scottish and African blood, he was tough, shrewd, prudent, decisive, personable, hard-working and far-sighted. He administered BC until 1864, and supervised its transition from fur trading empire to colony. In 1843 the HBC established a fort at Victoria on Vancouver Island, and begin preparing it as a potential headquarters. Victoria had the advantages of being easily protected by the Royal Navy which used the excellent harbour at Esquimalt a few kilometers away. It was near good agricultural land, and far north of the American posts. Some agriculture developed as well as a saw mill, and retired HBC employees began to settle down in and near the growing village of Victoria.

But the HBC could not counter the flood of American settlement surging west across the plains and into Oregon. Pressure mounted for statehood and for control of all land up to the border with Russian Alaska at 54' 40". In 1844 James Polk won the American presidential election partly on a promise to seize the entire Pacific coast, as epitomized in his campaign slogan "54'40" or Fight".

In fact, neither Polk nor the British wanted a war, and a diplomatic compromise was soon reached. The 49th parallel was extended from the Rockies to the coast and Britain retained all of Vancouver Island. The Americans thus gained the present-day state of Washington, but Britain retained 2/3 of the disputed coast, from south of present-day Vancouver to north of Prince Rupert, plus the entire interior north and east of that coast.

With the loss of Fort Vancouver and the lower Columbia, the HBC had to develop the more difficult transportation routes of the Fraser River. Fort Langley was established near the mouth of the Fraser, and a new fort was built at Fort Hope at the foot of the mountain passes. From there the HBC established a combination of water routes and land routes using pack animals. The fur trade was already in serious decline as beaver hats went out of style in Europe, and the added costs of transportation hastened the decline. But Britain wanted to safeguard its west coast possessions from further American encroachment, and to spend as little money as possible doing it. The only organization that was in a position to help was the HBC, and developing Vancouver Island gave it a new purpose and source of easy profit.

The small fort that had been established at Victoria in 1843 soon became the base for all HBC operations in the region. It had been growing slowly to service the trade along the west coast, which was handled by the steamboat *The Beaver* from 1835 until 1875. Victoria also served as a supply base for Pacific trade. The British fleet was beginning to use nearby Esquimalt as a base, which added considerable demand for food, lumber and coal as well as an element of elegance to the fledgling social life of the colony. Agriculture slowly expanded around the base. Lumber was exported to California and salmon to Hawaii, and the coal resources at Nanaimo were soon making a significant contribution to the growing economy.

In 1849 Britain established the colony of Vancouver Island and then immediately rented it to the HBC. The HBC's Chief Factor, James Douglas, soon became Governor combining the chief economic and political positions on the island, as well as being Chief Factor of the HBC on the mainland. The HBC was committed to bringing settlers to the island, but this plan was doomed because settlement threatened the very existence of a fur-trading company. Britain wanted to replicate its own stratified society, with a wealthy, patriotic and Anglican land-owning class of gentlemen farmers dominating their lower-class tenants. To keep out squatters, speculators and Americans, land was sold at one pound an acre, four times the price of land in the United States. The minimum purchase was 20 acres, and the buyer had to agree to settle five unmarried tenants or three married ones.

These conditions, the six month trip, the lack of neighbours, and the availability of free land and political rights elsewhere precluded any rapid development. Ninety percent of the revenue from land sales was to be spent on public works. But there was little revenue since few people bought land, and the lack of roads and bridges further discouraged settlement. The HBC managed to attract about half a dozen would-be squires who created a genteel society with fox hunts and fancy parties. Their relationship with Douglas was strained, partly because he and the HBC men wielded the real power, partly because he and the HBC men had Native wives and families. Some HBC employees settled with their Native wives and Metis children, now social outcasts of the haughty white gentry. Douglas recognized that the land belonged to the Natives, and negotiated 14 treaties to provide for the legal alienation of a small portion of Vancouver Island, but elsewhere no treaties were negotiated.

In 1856 Britain ordered Douglas to establish a representative legislative assembly. He grudgingly obeyed, but restricted the franchise to white males who owned at least 20 acres of land worth three hundred pounds. Only 43 residents qualified out of a population of around 500. They duly elected seven of themselves, almost all HBC men. Their meeting of August 12, 1856, constituted the first assembly in British North America west of Lake Ontario. The assembly did provide a check on Douglas' power, for example by refusing to approve any taxes and asking embarrassing questions about the accounts. The colonial government was also weakened by its attitudes, by British immigration policy, and by the shortage of revenue.

Chapter Three
Confederation, 1855-1871

On Sunday, 25 April 1858, the denizens of Victoria went to church as usual. By the time they emerged, the population of the tiny community had doubled with the arrival of 400 miners on their way to the Fraser River. Gold had been discovered, and they wanted some of it. Actually, it had been discovered years earlier, and the HBC had kept it a secret. But that spring the HBC had shipped 800 ounces to San Francisco, and the secret was out. By then the great California gold rush was over, and thousands of miners headed up the coast on any ship that could carry them, 10,000 by June, 25,000 by October and possibly 50,000 at the height of the gold rush in 1861.

The immediate beneficiaries of the invasion were the shopkeepers and landowners of Victoria. The miners had to buy provisions, and the number of stores doubled. Soon there were almost as many bars as there had been buildings a few months earlier, often providing gambling and brothels. The price of land skyrocketed, and the HBC made a fortune selling the land it was supposed to have provided to settlers. The population changed dramatically, from the domination of the HBC men and a few aspiring English gentry to a cosmopolitan mix of people from all over Europe and the United States plus Jews, blacks and Chinese. By December the population had exploded from 300 to 5,000, and in 1862 Victoria was incorporated as a city.

On the mainland, Douglas faced the problems of controlling the miners, and ensuring that they did not effect the annexation of BC to the United States. On Vancouver Island Douglas was Governor but on the mainland he was only Chief Factor of the HBC, a position with no legal political power. But Douglas was a man of sound judgment and decisiveness. The situation could not wait for Britain to sort out the legal niceties and send instructions half way around the world. He acted as though he had the authority of governor, and left the legitimization of his actions for later.

Douglas immediately asserted that all land on the mainland and therefore all mines on it belonged to the British crown. To mine for gold one therefore needed a licence from the crown, namely from him, and it cost two dollars. That forced the miners to come through Victoria and accept, in effect, British sovereignty over the mainland. Douglas moved quickly to establish law and order by appointing a number of district judges, who went on horseback from mining camp to mining camp, sorting out disputes, judging guilt and innocence, and meting out harsh sentences in order to discourage further trouble. These magistrates were soon backed up by British Royal Engineers, who were also responsible for building roads and bridges, and by the Royal Navy, which reminded the Americans that BC and Vancouver Island were not available for annexation.

As a result of Douglas's swift action, the degree of violence in BC was significantly less than that on the American frontier and in the mining camps. Considerable violence occurred when miners violated Native hunting and fishing areas, and the miners then welcomed British law and order to protect them from the revenge of the Natives. Douglas made Victoria a free port and imposed a 10% tariff on all goods going to the mainland. That ensured that Victoria controlled trade and commerce and had the revenue to finance the public works necessitated by the rapid growth in population. Douglas also banned American boats from the rivers. That reinforced British sovereignty along with the HBC monopoly on river transportation, as Douglas continued to serve his two masters simultaneously and well.

With minimal law and order ensured, the miners could struggle up the rivers in search of instant fortune. Over the centuries gold flakes had been leached out of ancient rock, washed down rushing rivers, and buried in layers of "gold dust" in the sand bars, often accompanied by nuggets the size of small stones. Gold could be extracted from the sand by swirling water over it in a pan until the heavier gold settled to the bottom. Anyone could do it, and tens of thousands tried. When one miner struck it rich, others soon gathered around that claim. When findings tailed off, they moved upstream, gradually working their way into the fabled Cariboo country, and eventually into much of the BC interior.

As the miners moved upriver, small towns sprang up to provide for their needs. They contained a basic range of services – assay offices to purchase the gold, banks, hardware and grocery stores, livery stables, a church and cemetery, and especially bars and brothels. The most famous town was Barkerville, which may have had a population of 10,000 at its height. But as the gold deposits were depleted in each area, the inhabitants followed the miners to the next boom town leaving a string of ghost towns along the route.

Better transportation was one of the greatest needs of the miners. Steamships soon plied the lower Fraser and the navigable rivers and lakes in the interior. Royal Engineers were sent out from England to build roads where rapids rendered river transportation impossible. They built roads from Harrison Lake to Lillooet, and the famous Cariboo Trail over the 600 kilometers from Yale to Barkerville, parts of it blasted out of hard rock or built on log trestles over crevices, gorges and rivers. They also surveyed land, laid out town sites, and helped maintain law and order.

The British government was pleased with the way Douglas had taken control of the fast-moving developments. The mainland needed a governor, and he had acted like one. Britain now had to adjust New Caledonia's status to conform to the new political reality that Douglas had created. On 2 August 1858 it was made a crown colony. Since there was already a French colony called Caledonia, Queen Victoria named the new one British Columbia, to make clear that the northern half of the Columbia River basin was British and not American. Worried that the gold seekers might venture into the Peace River country which was then part of the HBC domain of Rupert's Land, Britain transferred that region to the colony of BC. The 120th meridian became the eastern border of BC from the Rockies north to the 60th degree of latitude. BC thus obtained a corner of the prairies and the Arctic tundra to add to its geographic variety.

Douglas was made governor of the colony of BC in addition to being Governor of the colony of Vancouver Island. But he now had to give up his other title of HBC Chief Factor. At the same time, the trading monopoly of the HBC was cancelled. On the mainland, the Royal Engineers selected a site for a new capital on the north bank of the Fraser. It was given the auspicious name of New Westminster. Lots were surveyed, trees felled, and speculators rushed in on the assumption that fortunes would be made as it became the capital of a great province. They were soon to be disappointed.

While all this frantic activity was unfolding on the mainland, Vancouver Island was developing a functioning Legislative Assembly. Effective power was still wielded by the British Government through Governor Douglas and a group of men, the Legislative Council or Cabinet, appointed by him. They held on to power because they did not trust the people to elect competent politicians and they did not personally like the ones who were elected. Most of the members of the Assembly were appointed, so Douglas could usually get the support of a majority. But the elected ones constantly criticized the Council for looking after its own interests. Petitions were regularly dispatched to London asking for the establishment of responsible and representative government. Just as regularly, they were ignored. But Douglas and the English elite did not always get their way – an attempt to create an established, government-subsidized Anglican Church failed.

On the mainland, Britain appointed Douglas and a Legislative Council or Cabinet to administer the colony. It did not create a Legislative Assembly for fear that Americans would dominate it and demand annexation to the United States. However, it soon became clear that Britain could not afford two administrations, especially since the Councilors in Victoria kept lavishing expenditure on themselves. By the mid-60s the gold rush had run its course, leaving both colonies with declining population and revenue, heavy debts from the public works, stagnant economies, and an uncertain future. Vancouver Island, in fact, was in such difficult financial straits that it demanded union with the mainland.

On 19 November, 1866, Britain announced the union of the two colonies. Though Vancouver Island was older and more established, the interests of the mainland prevailed in the union. The name of the new colony was British Columbia. The capital was to be on the mainland. Victoria lost the duty-free status which had given it a 10% advantage over the mainland. The Island lost its Legislative Assembly, and none was established in the new colony. The new Legislative Council contained four representatives elected on the Island, five elected on the mainland, six appointed officials and nine appointed magistrates. To mollify the Island's outrage, the council voted 14 to five to make Victoria the capital, the five opposing being the elected members from the mainland.

The new colonial government made some progress establishing administration, especially through ten Gold Commissioners who performed a wide range of government services. The economy remained weak but gradually diversified, based on coal and gold mining, logging and saw milling, fishing, ranching and farming. The non-Native population increased from around 1,000 before the gold rush to 10,000 a decade later. Land policy continued to hamper agriculture as there was no requirement to develop land after it was claimed. In New Westminster, for example, only one-third of surveyed land was claimed, and only one-hundredth of that was farmed, the rest being kept off the market for speculation.

The government's biggest failure was probably with Native policy. It was widely assumed that the Natives would simply disappear as a result of disease and assimilation. Indeed, between the gold rush and Confederation the Native population probably declined by half, and many of the survivors did enter the white economy as labourers, fishermen and loggers. The government hastened both trends by taking back much of the land that had been set aside for Natives and decreeing that a Native family could live on 10 acres of land when the amount on the prairies was 160 acres.

As the economy continued to stagnate, a small group of immigrants from Canada and the Maritimes began to argue that BC should join the amalgamated colony that was being created in the eastern third of British North America. The motives of this pro-confederation group were mainly personal, financial and even social. They had been shut out of government jobs and high society by the dominant English and HBC elite. They assumed that they would replace that elite if BC became a Canadian province with responsible government. They were also businessmen, and Confederation would bring access to markets and an end to economic stagnation. Leaders soon emerged such as Amor de Cosmos, born Bill Smith. He was the aggressive editor of the *British Colonist*, a Victoria newspaper that constantly attacked Douglas and his government for various sins real and imagined but invariably exaggerated. In New Westminster, John Robson carried out similar attacks in his journal, *The British Columbian.*

The majority of white British Columbians were, however, opposed to Confederation, and the vast majority of inhabitants, the Natives, had no voice at all. Canada was many thousands of miles away, beyond the vast lands of the HBC. The English and HBC elite were fearful that Confederation would do what the Canadian faction wanted, namely, transfer power to Canadians. They liked the genteel English society they had created and dominated, and had no desire to weaken British institutions or connections. Since transportation was by ship around Cape Horn, BC was almost as close to London as to Montreal. Another small but noisy faction wanted annexation to the United States.

In the new Canada many people envisioned a colony stretching from sea to sea, with the prairies and BC as an economic hinterland to be exploited for the growing industry of Ontario and Quebec. Britain was also in favour of the concept of Confederation that was being developed in Canada and the Maritimes. The amalgamation of its seven North American colonies and territories into a single colony stretching from Atlantic to Pacific could block American expansionism, and such a colony would be better able to defend itself. Britain supported the union of Canada (Quebec and Ontario) with New Brunswick and Nova Scotia in 1867, and helped arrange for Canada to purchase Rupert's Land from the HBC. That brought Canada to BC's eastern border. Britain then began to pressure BC to join Confederation. The issue became urgent when the United States bought Alaska from Russia in 1867.

The Canadian Prime Minister, John A. Macdonald, arranged for Britain to appoint a new pro-Confederation Governor, Anthony Musgrave. His mandate was to bring about BC's entry into Confederation. He quickly realized that the inhabitants had no sentimental attachment to Canada, no great fear of the United States, and no political reason for trading their status as a single British colony for subordinate provincial status in a huge and potentially unwieldy British colony. Fortunately the bloodbath of the American Civil War had dampened enthusiasm for annexation, and those who wished BC to remain a separate British colony soon discovered that Britain did not share that goal.

Musgrave advanced the cause of union with Canada by helping to draft a set of conditions that Ottawa was to accept in order to entice the reluctant colony to join. It was a negotiating position, so it asked as much as the politicians dared. As such it received unanimous approval in the Assembly. It asked the federal Canadian government to assume the colony's huge debt, give it an annual per capita subsidy based on a population estimated at three times the actual population, pay pensions to officials who were not retained, build public works including a wagon trail and telegraph from Lake Superior, and start spending one million dollars annually on a railway within three years and complete it as soon as possible. Musgrave selected the delegates who took a steamer to San Francisco and a railway across the United States and up to Ottawa. Canadian Prime Minister Macdonald was ill so the delegation met his chief lieutenant, George Etienne Cartier.

To the surprise of the delegates, Cartier accepted almost all of BCs demands. Ottawa promised a huge annual subsidy and agreed to pay the annual interest on the cost of building a dry dock at Esquimalt. There were to be six MPs and three Senators, far more than the population justified. But to their further amazement, Cartier promised a railway, to be started in two years and completed in ten. BC was to give the federal government a strip of land 20 miles wide on both sides of the proposed railway in return for an annual grant of $100,000 in perpetuity. Finally, the responsibility and costs of Native policy were transferred to Ottawa. The delegates returned to Victoria in triumph, with terms that far exceeded their wildest hopes. Musgrave took advantage of the euphoria to call an election for the nine elected members of the Council. Pro-Confederation candidates easily won every seat.

While BC celebrated the marvelous deal, cooler heads in Ottawa wondered why Cartier had promised to build a railway and whether Canada could afford it. The Liberal Opposition was completely opposed. Conservative MPs in Macdonald's government sensed that the offer was financially impossible and perhaps politically suicidal. Fortunately one of the BC delegates, Joseph Trutch, happened to be back in Ottawa. Without any authority from the BC government, he assured the Conservative MPs that BC did not expect Canada to bankrupt itself to honour the terms. With this assurance, the Conservative MPs passed the bill admitting BC to Confederation.

On 20 July 1871 BC became Canada's sixth province, Manitoba having joined the original four provinces in 1870. In half a dozen years the colonies of Canada, New Brunswick and Nova Scotia had combined into one, acquired the whole of Rupert's Land, and seduced British Columbia into joining Confederation. The new colony now stretched from Atlantic to Pacific, and *from sea to sea* would later become its motto. But BC joined on the understanding that a railway was to be started in two years and completed in ten, while Ottawa understood that the promise of a railway could be broken with impunity.

Soon the promise was, indeed, broken, and the joys of 1871 turned to anger and then to demands to secede from Canada. What was particularly puzzling about the negotiations is that BC was given more than it requested, while at Red River an equally large group of colonists had to rebel to obtain far less. BC retained control of its natural resources; those of Manitoba and later Alberta and Saskatchewan were retained by the federal government. BC retained its colonial borders making it the third largest province; Manitoba was limited in size to an area little bigger than the Fraser delta. In 1871 BC entered Canada in such a privileged position that it soon came to be known as the "spoilt child of Confederation". But that is not how BC saw it, and the violation of the promise to build the railway poisoned the relationship between Victoria and Ottawa. It left a feeling that BC, like the prairies, had been mistreated and cheated. Decades later BC premiers were still drawing on that anti-Ottawa sentiment. Indeed, it has never completely disappeared.

Chapter Four

Broken Promises and Threats of Secession, 1871-1885

Once British Columbia joined Canada there was no reason to continue withholding responsible government. The new Canadian-appointed Lieutenant-Governor, Joseph Trutch, duly dismissed the old Legislative Council with its nine elected and fifteen appointed members. New elections were called for a Legislative Assembly in which all 25 of the Members or MLAs would be elected for a maximum four-year term and would remain "responsible" to their electors.

Trutch then selected one of the MLAs, John Foster McCreight, to be the province's first premier. He in turn selected four fellow MLAs to constitute the first Cabinet. They were "responsible" to the Assembly, not the lieutenant governor, and could carry on the tasks of government only as long as they had the support of a majority of the MLAs. When premiers left, which was fairly frequent, another MLA took over, probably kept most of the same cabinet, and continued to govern. If that clique lost an election, another group formed the government, usually with some of the same members, usually pursuing the same policies. Finally BC had responsible, democratic, non-partisan government. This was the same system as that of the future Alberta and Saskatchewan, where it worked very well for decades.

Many people in BC had also demanded representative government, a system in which each MLA would represent roughly the same number of voters. The new Assembly no longer contained appointed members, and that automatically made it far more representative of the population. But it was still far from being truly representative, and would become even less so in coming decades. All male subjects could vote, providing they were 21 years of age, had lived in a constituency for six months, and were literate. As in the rest of the democratic world, women would not get the vote for another half century. Natives made up the vast majority of the population, but the Assembly took away their vote in 1874 along with that of the Chinese. When immigration from Japan increased, the vote was taken away from them in 1895 and later from the East Indians in 1907. In 1884 the literacy and property qualifications were abolished, ensuring the vote for all white, male, adult British subjects.

The newly-elected MLAs soon discovered the political advantages of re-arranging constituency borders to enhance their own chances of re-election. Thus was born the practice of ensuring that constituencies that elected pro-government MLAs had fewer electors while ones that tended to vote against the government had many. At first, Vancouver Island elected far more MLAs, 12 out of 25, than it deserved. From the beginning, rural MLAs managed to ensure that it took fewer rural voters to elect an MLA than it did urban voters, a situation that has never changed. That system helps explain the fact that established governments have been re-elected far more often than they have been defeated, often obtaining two-thirds or more of the seats in the assembly on the strength of well under half the popular vote.

The government immediately went to work setting up Canada's newest province. Its tariffs and excise taxes were adjusted to the Canadian rates, and tolls were abolished on the Cariboo Trail. The British civil service was replaced with a Canadian one, a regular judiciary established and municipalities mapped out. The government adopted rules to govern the Legislative Assembly and introduced the secret ballot for elections. A free, universal non-sectarian education system was created.

In 1870 Ottawa had bought BC, but it had not yet paid for it. The main form of payment was to be a transcontinental railway, to be started in 1873 and completed by 1881. In order for construction to start on time, surveying had to begin almost immediately. When no surveyors appeared, those who were skeptical about Ottawa's overly generous terms began to think that the province had been duped. Newspapers argued that if the terms were not met, then the province's agreement to enter on those terms was equally invalid, and the province could and should secede.

The demand that Ottawa honour its promises soon dominated provincial politics. It remained the dominant issue for a decade, because immediate construction was necessary to revive the economy, and future prosperity depended overwhelmingly on the opening of the interior and the linkage to eastern Canada. The question of railway construction soon became enmeshed in a series of related issues connecting federal and provincial politics, economics, finances, business, geography and surveying. The first question that had to be resolved was what route to survey from the coast to the interior, a question that was as much political as it was geographic or economic.

Victoria had dominated the region since 1841. It was determined to maintain its status, which meant that Victoria or Esquimalt would have to be the western terminal of the transcontinental railway. From there it would run north through Nanaimo, over the Georgia Strait on a series of bridges to Bute Inlet, and inland over the Chilcotin Plateau to connect with the line coming over the Rockies. Economically this proposal made little sense. The logical route was up the Fraser from Burrard Inlet, the route preferred by the half of the population that lived on the mainland. That meant that the population and the government of BC were almost evenly divided over the question of the two routes.

John A. Macdonald and his Conservative Government made little effort to begin surveying in the first two years. The dispute within BC over the route gave them an excuse to procrastinate, for how could detailed surveying begin if the overall route had not been agreed? Then in 1873 the opposition Liberals who had always opposed the railway came to power in Ottawa. Their arrival coincided with the beginning of an economic depression which doubly reinforced their desire to delay the plans for railway construction.

The new Liberal Prime Minister, Alexander Mackenzie, then asked BC to renegotiate the contract that had brought BC into confederation, that is, to provide "better terms" for the federal government. BC was asked, in effect, to forget the railway for a while and accept instead a carriageway and a telegraph plus a railway sometime in the future. Once the survey was completed, for which no date was offered, Ottawa would begin building the railway at the rather slow rate produced by an expenditure of $1.5 million per year. If these terms were not acceptable to BC, Ottawa would build a railway from Esquimalt to Nanaimo instead, an offer that divided Island politicians from those from the mainland.

An infuriated Premier George Walkem took BC's grievances immediately to London, because PM Mackenzie's new terms clearly violated the terms of union that Britain had helped negotiate between Canada and British Columbia. In January 1874 BC backed up its case with a threat to secede, a motion that carried unanimously in the Assembly. A worried British Colonial Secretary, Lord Carnarvon, offered to mediate, which infuriated Ottawa as it believed that relations between federal and provincial governments were now an internal Canadian matter.

Ignoring Ottawa's view, Carnarvon proposed a new set of terms: building the Esquimalt-Nanaimo railway immediately, speeding up the surveys, immediate construction of a wagon trail and telegraph, and the completion of the railway by 1890. Ottawa then made a counter-proposal: no Esquimalt-Nanaimo railway, $750,000 as compensation for the delay, and $250,000 for a dry-dock which Ottawa had also promised in 1871 but about which nothing had been done. BC rejected these terms and threatened again to secede. In Ottawa British Governor General, Lord Dufferin, attempted to intervene, but Mackenzie rejected his counsel.

The federal offer of $750,000 dollars annually in lieu of the broken promise was disingenuous. The relevant legal document contained no time-frame, making it unclear as to whether it was only compensation for past delays, or for past, present and future delays. Lord Dufferin disagreed sharply with Mackenzie over it. Mackenzie also made further promises that were contradictory, saying that he would build the railway but not if it meant going into debt. Since it would definitely go into debt, he was both promising to build it and saying he wouldn't. Governor Dufferin, a man of considerable integrity, felt that the federal government had lost its credibility on the issue. He asked London to mediate, but London refused. In 1878 BC sent another petition to London threatening to secede.

The 1878 federal election returned Sir John A. Macdonald's Conservatives to power, with building the transcontinental as the government's top priority. The contract was given to the Canadian Pacific Railway, the CPR. The decision was finally made to put the Pacific terminus somewhere on Burrard Inlet, and Victoria was doomed to become BC's second city. With agreement that the western half of the route would go up the Fraser, the next question was where it would go through the Rockies. The Crowsnest route between Trail and southern Alberta was quickly ruled out because the grades were too steep and it was too close to the United States. From BC's perspective, the best route in terms of grades and centrality to the province was the Yellowhead, coming west from Edmonton to Jasper, over to the Thompson River and down to Kamloops. It also had the advantage of being surveyed and proven.

Instead, the CPR decided to build the railway across the southern prairies, which meant that it had to go through the Rockies somewhere west of Calgary. At the time the decision was made, no suitable pass had been found through the Rockies. Major A.B. Rogers was sent to find one. His crew struggled up the Bow River from Calgary, towards Golden and Revelstoke. He found the Kicking Horse Pass and the pass named after him. But he miscalculated the grades, possibly because he was not given enough time to complete proper surveys. For decades the CPR would have to put extra engines on the trains and pay the costs of numerous train wrecks.

It was decided to build the railroad simultaneously from the east across the prairies and over the Rockies, and from Yale up the Fraser River Canyon. On 14 May 1880 construction began on the BC portion at Yale. Macdonald's arrangement with the CPR did not include the Esquimalt-Nanaimo railway which had been promised several times, so the BC Assembly passed another resolution by a vote of twenty to four asking again for British intervention.

Still genuinely worried that BC might secede and join the United States, Britain asked Macdonald to be more flexible. Instead, Macdonald made new demands on Victoria. In the original deal BC had given Ottawa a twenty-mile strip of land on each side of the railway for Ottawa to use as enticement to get a private company to build the line. But much of that land was mountainous, and Macdonald demanded that BC swap it for 3,500,000 acres of good agricultural land in the Peace River district. To show its annoyance with Ottawa, Victoria re-imposed tolls on the Cariboo Trail over which the CPR was transporting the supplies needed for construction.

Having delayed construction for ten years, Ottawa was now in a hurry to complete it as soon as possible. White labour could be found to build the eastern portion, over thousands of miles from Lake Superior to Revelstoke, including the most difficult section over the Rockies. But the CPR contractor for the western portion, Andrew Onderdonk, claimed there was insufficient white labour to build his short section. The solution to that problem, he argued, was to import Chinese workers. Chinese workers could also be paid wages far lower than white workers and were willing to live in terrible conditions.

Chinese had been present in BC since the days of the gold rush. These new workers were recruited in China by employment companies. The poor wages they received greatly exceeded those in China, and a dozen years of hard labour and privation would allow them to return to China and lead a relatively good life. By 1884 an estimated 15,000 Chinese workers had entered BC, and possibly 1,500 of them died from disease or accident while building the CPR.

The importation of Chinese labour immediately provoked an outcry in BC. In part, it was racial discrimination. Many whites did not want Asians in the province, including the smaller groups of Japanese and East Indians. Whites regarded Asians as racially inferior, thought they were heathen, did not like their customs, dress and eating habits, and feared that the Asian masses would swamp their comfortable, "superior" white civilization. Since the Chinese were poorly paid and wanted to save every dollar, they crowded into slums. Whites were concerned that such slums were a breeding ground for disease. Since the Chinese population was almost entirely single men, many of them spent their leisure time with gambling, opium and prostitution, and were therefore identified with immorality and crime.

Another concern for whites was the effects of low wages on the income of white workers. When white workers went on strike, they were sometimes replaced by scab Chinese labour. When whites tried to stop them, the provincial government sent police and troops to "maintain order", that is, to break the strikes. The CPR rapidly branched into mining, forestry and real estate, so it continued to benefit from the effects of Chinese labour on wages.

The BC Assembly quickly took steps to bar Chinese immigration. One law requiring companies to get a licence to use Chinese labour was disallowed by the federal government. BC imposed a poll tax which would have made it expensive to import Chinese men. That would have affected the CPR's construction schedule and costs, and the Supreme Court in Ottawa overturned the legislation. Ottawa also disallowed a $10 licence imposed by the province in 1878. BC passed more laws to bar Chinese workers; Ottawa used various methods to disallow or veto them.

The issue of Chinese labour and immigration replaced the broken railway promises as the main issue in BC's relations with the federal government, and dragged on for decades. After the completion of the railway, Ottawa acted on BC's demands, imposing a $50 head tax on new Chinese immigrants. This was raised to $100 in 1901 and $500 in 1904, and in 1923 the Chinese were excluded altogether. But Onderdonk's plan worked. On 7 November 1885 the last symbolic spike was driven in the CPR mainline at a whistle stop called Craigellachie just west of Revelstoke.

Construction also began on the western portion of the BC line, from Yale to Burrard Inlet. As usual, the CPR was building before it had fully surveyed the route or identified the major towns or ports. It followed this practice so that it could buy up the land as cheaply as possible before the new towns and cities created by the railway's arrival led to booms in real estate. As the line approached Burrard Inlet, it looked like the terminal would be at Port Moody, where the railway arrived in July, 1886. Speculators rushed in to buy up the choice lots. But Port Moody was not a good site for a harbour, and the CPR decided instead on a port near Granville or Gastown.

William Van Horne, President of the CPR, chose the name Vancouver in honour of the explorer, but to the annoyance of the denizens of the island with the same name. The provincial government donated 6,000 acres to the CPR, an unnecessary gift since the CPR had to build a terminal and had already decided on the site. Land speculators were so excited at the prospect of a great city in their region that they gave the CPR one-third of the land they had just bought. A gracious CPR accepted the unnecessary gifts, because real estate would become as important as rail freight to its enormous profits. The port was laid out, and on 23 May 1887 the first passenger train chugged into the new terminal.

With the main problems of building the railway resolved, the federal and provincial governments quickly settled other outstanding issues. BC gave the federal government the 3,500,000 acres it had demanded in the Peace River country in compensation for land along the CPR mainline. BC also gave one-third of Vancouver Island - 2,000,000 acres - to the federal government which gave that land plus $750,000 to a consortium headed by Robert Dunsmuir to build the Esquimalt-Nanaimo railway. Ottawa promised again to begin constructing the Esquimalt dry-dock. And, now that the CPR was almost completed, Ottawa promised to restrict Chinese immigration. With the province's capital now definitely sited in Victoria, the main grievances of the Island had been addressed. For a few years, both the Island and the mainland would be tranquil.

Chapter Five
Unsteady Progress, 1885-1900

The province's early development was handicapped by the inexperience of its politicians with their new political institutions. BC became a full-fledged province before it attained responsible government. Inevitably its politicians and administrators lacked the political experience to make those institutions work properly. From Confederation until the adoption of the party system in 1903, the province had fifteen different governments. In the first dozen years, six people occupied the premier's office, one of them on two separate occasions. Most of these administrations contained the same ministers, and most of them carried on with the same policies. They presided over the building of the railroads, the cities and the economy. With their efforts and BC's natural advantages, thousands of people settled in the new province. The population almost doubled in each of the next three decades, numbering 35,000 in 1871, 50,000 in 1881, 100,000 in 1891 and 180,000 in 1901. Significantly, non-Natives became a majority for the first time in the mid-1880s.

The effects of government instability have often been exaggerated. But changing premiers every few years was not conducive to dealing with the federal government which had only two prime ministers between 1867 and 1891. The musical chairs in the premier's office began with the first government. Lieutenant Governor Joseph Trutch selected John McCreight, a newly-elected MLA. In less than a year McCreight was replaced by Amor de Cosmos who had been in the previous assembly. But in two years he opted to be an MP in Ottawa, possibly to avoid questions about links between his governmental and his private interests. De Cosmos had been the greatest proponent of Confederation, but he became a separatist when Ottawa failed to build the railway.

George Walkem's faction won the election of 1875 but soon lost a vote of confidence in the Assembly. His replacement, Andrew Charles Elliott, was also defeated in the Assembly and then in the election in 1878. Walkem returned as premier until he was appointed to the BC Supreme Court, and his replacement, Robert Beaven, lost the 1882 election. Corruption, accidents and promotions also took a toll on BC's early premiers. In 1892 Premier John Robson visited London to attract investments. While there he caught his finger in the door of a taxi, got an infection, and died of blood poisoning. His successor, Theodore Davie, only served for three years before retiring to a quieter position on the BC Supreme Court.

Trutch was not the only lieutenant governor to have difficulty selecting premiers. After the election of 1898 Thomas McInnis decided that Premier John Turner no longer had the confidence of the Assembly even though there had been no vote. He inexplicably appointed Robert Beaven, who had been defeated in the election, had no support, and soon had to resign. McInnis then appointed Charles Semlin, and while he won a vote of confidence, his government soon fell apart. The lieutenant governor appointed the unpopular and abrasive Joseph Martin, who lost a confidence vote by 28 to one. When McInnis came to prorogue the Assembly, all the MLAs except Martin and the Speaker walked out. Martin governed for three months without the benefit of support in the Assembly. In just two years five different politicians had occupied the premier's chair.

In the meantime, railway construction produced the economic boom its promoters had predicted. A string of large towns grew up as divisional centres and repair yards – Yale, Golden, Kamloops, Revelstoke. The demand for ties, bridges, trestles, stations, and sidings produced the first real boom in the forest industry. The cost of transportation dropped, dramatically cutting the price of BC's exports and imports. The huge construction crews provided a market for agriculture and ranching, getting them launched on a permanent footing. The CPR immediately started a steamship line across the Pacific, and goods and people were soon travelling from Hong Kong to London via the CPR because it was the quickest route across North America. That provided permanent freight and hence permanent jobs along the line through BC.

Economic growth was perhaps best symbolized by the expansion of Vancouver, from a few houses in 1885 to incorporation as a city of 2,000 in 1886. It grew to 5,000 in 1887 and 14,000 in 1991, doubling again to 27,000 by 1901. By then it had miles of roads, electric trams, sewers and water mains, and the famous Stanley Park. Once the regional banks made Vancouver their head-quarters, major companies had to do the same. It became the centre of industry, with foundries, factories, flour mills, office buildings and hotels. Victoria's population had doubled between 1881 and 1891, but by 1900 it had lost the race to Vancouver.

But the BC government could not develop the province's economy on its own. All the big sectors of the economy – transportation, mining, forestry and canning – required large investments, and only big outside companies had the necessary capital, organization, personnel, technology and connections. The political culture of the time dictated that the economy be run by private business. The role of government was to provide law and order, basic administrative infrastructure such as city and municipal government, an education system that would produce people capable of filling jobs from mechanic to company president, some basic services, and the minimum laws required to regulate living and working conditions.

To ensure that private enterprise developed the economy and produced jobs and government revenue, the government had to provide transportation infrastructure and inducements to invest. The government had little money, but it did have millions of acres of valuable land. Its policy, therefore, was to give land to companies to entice them to invest in railways, mines, irrigation, or logging operations. This policy had started with the land grants to the CPR and to Robert Dunsmuir for the Esquimalt-Nanaimo railway. After the completion of the CPR in 1885, land grants became the main business of BC politics. Since land grants were so lucrative, MLAs could expect favours from the companies seeking them, but the MLAs and businessmen were all part of the same small coterie of people whose goals were the economic development of the province and their personal enrichment. As in the days of the HBC, business and government remained almost one and the same, as summed up in the popular saying that the CPR was the province's government on wheels.

Steamboats provided transportation on the lakes and navigable rivers of the interior, but railways were essential to link the regions to each other and the outside world. To build them major companies like the CPR were given millions of acres of land. Banking on future profit in land sales and exploitation, they then borrowed the money to build branch lines south into the Okanagan and the Kootenays, and later to connect the Kootenays with southern Alberta through the Crowsnest Pass. Small companies and companies that existed solely on paper soon found that MLAs were eager to grant charters with millions of acres of timber, agricultural land, and potential town sites.

When many of these railways failed to materialize, large companies like the CPR bought up their charters and land grants, added these to existing holdings, built the railways, and make fortunes selling the land or exploiting the timber and mineral resources on it. Charges of waste, extravagance and corruption regularly rocked the province, and some politicians were disgraced for failing to adequately disguise their activities. But in fact, the private companies did come to BC, they did build the railways, they did invest in mining and forestry, and the province grew steadily because of the basic policy of land grants.

Fishing developed rapidly once the technology of canning opened the markets of Europe to BC salmon. The canning industry required large investments partly because of the equipment needed and partly because the salmon spawned in a pattern that saw one bumper year followed by several leaner years, and rich companies could better survive those lean years. As the industry grew, the larger companies absorbed the smaller ones until a few giants dominated. The workforce was ethnically-and sexually-based, with Japanese and white men dominating fishing while Native women and Chinese men provided much of the labour in the canneries.

In 1901 the companies decided to lower the price they paid to the fishermen. That provoked a strike, which was broken by the militia and by the decision by Japanese fishermen to accept the lower price. The increasing Japanese presence in the fishing industry created resentment in the white population, and the pattern of government intervention by force on the side of the companies helped radicalize labour. Over-fishing became a problem, and governments began attempts at regulation.

The Nanaimo coal mines were an important but controversial part of the Vancouver Island economy for decades. The ruthless owner, Robert Dunsmuir, was infamous for refusing to invest in safety or to pay decent wages and for forcing the workers to live in cheap housing and pay extravagant prices at the company store. His mines were notorious for deaths, injuries and strikes. He broke strikes by using scab workers, and relied on the government to send the militia to control violence. On the mainland the main centre of mining was the Kootenays, which were soon producing copper, lead, zinc, silver and gold. By 1900 over half of Canada's mineral wealth came from BC. At first American and British companies dominated, but the CPR rapidly bought up the mines. Its mining interests eventually became the giant Cominco company, linked to other mines, the CPR's own forests for timber, and its dominant position in the region's transportation networks. Trail, Kimberley, Nelson, Fernie, and Rossland became the centres of the mining and smelting industry.

BC had been exporting timber and lumber since the mid-nineteenth century, but the forestry industry developed slowly due to distance from markets. The construction of the CPR created a short boom, and the industry grew slowly thereafter, providing lumber and timber to the mines and railways and for residential, business and factory construction. The government attempted to stimulate logging with virtually no regulation and cheap leases. As demand increased and larger logging companies emerged from consolidation, the government gradually improved regulations and increased the cost of leases. The real boom in the forest industry resulted from the settlement of the prairies after 1896, a boom which finally allowed the government to regain control over land, impose better regulations to control the forests, and begin collecting substantial revenues from the resource.

Agriculture developed into a minor but still important sector of the BC economy. Less than 5% of the province was arable, most of it in small bands along river valleys. The rich Fraser delta soon specialized in market gardening and dairy products for the Vancouver market. Conditions were near-perfect for fruit farming in the Okanagan, and BC apples soon became a staple food in eastern Canada and the UK. Ranching expanded with the demands of the CPR construction crews, and remained a significant industry due to the excellent conditions in the dry interior of the province. BC agriculture often required expensive investment in ranches, irrigation in the dry interior or drainage near the rain-soaked coast. Successful farming was therefore more capital-intensive than on the prairies, and farmers were often drawn from the wealthier class. The largest agricultural region and the only one suitable for wheat was the remote Peace River area, but it was not opened for settlement until well into the twentieth century.

The federal government contributed to the province's growth, particularly with the development of the essential transportation infrastructure. But Ottawa's biggest failure was with Native policy. Although Governor Douglas had negotiated a few treaties on Vancouver Island, that practice ended when he was replaced and no treaties were negotiated on the mainland. This problem was not addressed when the federal government took responsibility for Natives in 1867. On the newly-acquired prairies Ottawa accepted that the Natives had sovereignty over the land, and negotiated treaties in which that sovereignty was traded for reserves, annual grants, and the equipment necessary to become farmers.

In BC, the province retained ownership of most of the land. The government in Victoria had been taking land away from the Natives in the 1860s, giving it to white settlers and companies such as the canneries who got control of the best fishing sites. This practice continued after Ottawa assumed responsibility for the Natives, and Ottawa was either unable or unwilling to intervene. BC's ownership of the land was part of the problem, but BC had transferred 13,000,000 acres of land to Ottawa to support railway construction. In fact, both governments failed to deal with the Natives' legal and land problems.

Ottawa turned the education of Natives over to missionaries who trained them for the worst jobs in white society and used corporal punishment to maintain discipline. Native children were taken from their families and put in distant residential schools which had the dual purpose of destroying their culture and preparing them for assimilation into white society. Discipline was harsh, and Native culture was weakened but not destroyed.

Natives fell farther behind whites in schooling, leading to increased poverty and marginalization. Ottawa outlawed potlatches because they violated the white work ethic and capitalist values, and Christian missionaries believed they preserved an inferior culture. The Natives continued the practice secretly in spite of great efforts by the churches and government to ban it, and in 1951 the discriminatory law was finally rescinded. As a result of these policies Natives were partly assimilated into the white economy, where they worked in the canneries, fishing, and logging, but they kept their native culture. The failure to negotiate treaties and settle land claims has plagued the province ever since.

In 1898 gold was discovered in the Klondike region of the Yukon Territory, to the north of BC. It touched off another mad stampede as tens of thousands of men sought instant fortunes. Servicing their needs created a short economic boom in Victoria, Vancouver and up the coast. The gold rush also forced the resolution of the last BC boundary dispute. The Alaskan Panhandle stretched one-third of the way down the west coast of BC, to a point just north of Prince Rupert. The border between it and BC was to follow the summits of the coastal mountains, but the line had never been demarcated.

That became important when the Klondike miners crossed the Alaskan Panhandle into BC on their way to the Yukon. If the border was near the coast, then the headwaters of the inlets would be Canadian. If the border was farther inland, the headwaters would be American, and Americans could control and tax the miners giving Seattle rather than Vancouver the benefits of the economic boom. The border dispute went to international arbitration, and in 1903 a line was drawn giving the United States the headwaters and roughly two-thirds of the disputed territory. Canadians saw it as another example of Britain sacrificing Canadian land for better relations with the United States. In fact, the boom was over and the American claim had been better, and all of BC's borders were now fixed. And as the nineteenth century came to an end, the province was becoming a little less British and a little more Canadian in sentiment, population, and economic and political linkages.

Chapter Six

The Great Boom, 1900-1914

The turn of the century witnessed profound change in British Columbia. One of the greatest economic booms in world history swept the province. The political system was changed fundamentally when the traditional party system replaced non-partisan politics. After experiencing over a dozen premiers in the first 30 years, one young politician, Richard McBride, came to dominate the province for a decade and a half. In ten years immigrants doubled the population, once more changing the ethnic, religious and cultural fabric. Railways branched out into new regions, opening up their economies, contributing to the economic boom, spawning hundreds of new cities and towns, and knitting the province together. Until shattered by the outbreak of World War I, the opening years of the twentieth century were the golden age of British Columbia.

The boom that transformed BC started in 1896 with the discovery of vast quantities of gold in South Africa. Almost all the conditions that had retarded the opening of the Canadian prairies changed, and spectacular growth there provided a huge market for BC lumber and other products. The boom in Central Canadian industry demanded resources from BC. Europe experienced unprecedented prosperity, creating further demand for BC's exports. Cheap and abundant capital poured into BC to finance new mines, industries, buildings and transportation facilities. Limited economic prospects and deteriorating political conditions in England and Europe prompted millions of immigrants to seek more peaceful lands, and many of them came to BC.

The framework for BC's economic growth was well established when the boom started. Railways and steamships linked the main regions, valleys, cities, and industries of the southern interior to each other, to the rest of Canada and to the United States. Port facilities were well developed. The basic pattern of the economy was clear, with fishing and canning along the coast, mining in numerous areas like the Kootenays, agriculture in the valleys and especially the Lower Mainland and Okanagan, forestry everywhere, service centres in the booming towns, and a growing financial and industrial heartland in Vancouver. Government infrastructure provided a basic level of transportation, education, municipal government, support to the private sector, and rules and regulations. In the next 15 years the economy tripled in size, and became more diversified and modern.

At the same time, the political system underwent a revolution that took it from the post-Confederation non-partisan system to one based on political parties. For thirty years after Confederation the loose coalitions of like-minded politicians gave the province the basic infrastructure it needed. They were criticized for excessive grants of land to private companies, but land was the most important incentive they had to attract private industry. Private companies did come, and the economy flourished because of their investments. The establishment of the party system did not change that basic approach to economic development.

Indeed, BC had a higher rate of economic growth than any other province in the last three decades of the nineteenth century and the second highest rate after the prairies in the early twentieth century. That was partly because a frontier economy requires massive investment in infrastructure at the same time as it is attracting massive investment in resources. BC had the highest wages in Canada, and the highest proportion of the population in the work force. It also had the highest ratio of men to women, the lowest ratio of children, and a comparatively young population.

By 1903, however, non-partisan government was no longer adequate to administer a diverse and rapidly-growing province. The breakdown was evident in the failure before 1903 to deal adequately with unions, finances, land grants, and regulations for labour and capital. It was evident in the succession of five different premiers between 1898 and 1903, and in the failure of Cabinet to put broad provincial interests ahead of regional interests.

It was also evident in the corruption of government. Two Cabinet Ministers had to resign over questionable land grants to railway companies. Premier E.G. Prior owned a hardware company that sold copper wire. As a member of the Cabinet he checked the bids on a huge contract for copper wire. Then as company owner he submitted a lower bid, which he as premier then accepted. The lieutenant governor viewed this as a conflict of interest and dismissed him.

Political decorum also broke down. Richard McBride had been elected leader of the opposition, but Joseph Martin desperately wanted the position. When the assembly met, McBride duly took his place in the opposition leader's seat. When the MLAs rose to hear the opening prayer, Martin slipped into McBride's seat, and as prayers were ending, McBride inadvertently sat down on him. A fist fight broke out. McBride won both the fight and another vote to be opposition leader, and was positioned for a bright future.

Although BC politicians were non-partisan provincially, many of them were aligned to either the Conservatives or the Liberal parties nationally. In 1902 a group of politicians who were Liberals federally held a convention and adopted a platform on which they would all run in the next provincial election. Later that year a group of Conservatives did the same. But the actual transition to party politics came about as the result of the political maneuverings of one man, Richard McBride. In 1902 he suddenly resigned from the Cabinet, and was elected leader by the opposition MLAs, most of whom were Liberals. Asked to form a government in 1903, he accepted, and announced that his government was Conservative.

"Glad-Hand Dick" as his critics called him, was elected to the Assembly in 1898 at the age of 33. His intelligence, charm, confidence and ability propelled him immediately into Cabinet. His mother was Catholic, his father Protestant, and he was at home with the rich or the working class. McBride was already in such a dominating leadership position that the politicians who had organized the Conservative party had to rally round him. He called an election and his new party won 22 of 42 seats. The Liberals then formed the opposition, and the two-party system was established.

With the economy booming and the new political system in place, BC was ready to receive the wave of immigration that would double its population from 200,000 in 1901 to 400,000 in 1911. The old British element that had dominated Victoria was reinforced by massive immigration from the British Isles. It consisted of three national or ethnic groups, the English, the Irish and the Scottish. They shared the language and political system, but they were quite different in culture, and represented different classes and occupations. In religion they were mainly Anglican, Catholic, Presbyterian, and Methodist. British immigrants were concentrated in government, teaching, the professions, management, ranching, fruit farming and the trades. In Victoria the English clung to their tradition of high society, proper manners, private schools, high tea at the Empress Hotel, and a preference for cricket, croquet, and British newspapers. When the Boer War erupted in South Africa in 1898, volunteers rushed off to save the British Empire, a clear reflection of where their sentiments and loyalties lay.

Immigrants continued to come from Ontario and the Maritimes, some born in the British Isles, many first or second-generation Canadians. Canadians were already sufficiently numerous and powerful to have dominated the debate over Confederation in the 1860s. They began arriving in significant numbers after the completion of the CPR in 1885, and by 1900 BC was clearly becoming more "Canadian" and less "British". The difference was subtle, though, as Canada remained very British, culturally and ideologically as demonstrated by massive support for Britain in World War I. The rest of Canada has been one of the largest sources of immigration ever since. Americans were never a major group after the gold rush, and were assimilated into the British-Canadian culture. Their culture, however, has had a lasting impact in a less traditional approach to politics, and a more aggressive and optimistic approach to business.

Many of the Chinese workers who had come to build the railway stayed in the province, finding work in low-paying service industries such as laundry and restaurants. But many returned to China, leaving a population of about 14,000 in 1901. Then their numbers began to increase rapidly, producing immediate demands to limit their immigration which the provincial government attempted to meet. The federal government was caught between the demands of workers and racists to restrict Asian immigration and the demand of businessmen to allow it. Ottawa compromised, raising the $50 head taxes imposed in 1885 to $100 in 1900 and $500 in 1904, and finally excluding all Chinese immigration in 1923.

Japanese began arriving in the 1890s, and they numbered 4,500 by 1900. They concentrated on the fishing industry, where they soon owned one-quarter of the boats. The Japanese aroused some of the same fears as did the Chinese, especially with their willingness to work for low wages and to break strikes, which depressed wages for white workers. In 1895 BC denied them the vote. Serious anti-Asian rioting in Vancouver in 1907 prompted Ottawa to negotiate an agreement with the Japanese government to limit immigration to 1,000 annually, later reduced to 400. In 1910 Ottawa passed a law stating that immigrants could only come by direct voyage. It was designed to end the smuggling of Japanese through Hawaii, and had the added effect of ending all emigration from India. But before then a small East Indian community had developed in the forestry industry, composed mainly of Sikhs who were often incorrectly called Hindus.

The fear of being swamped by Asians was exaggerated because the immigrants were mainly males and many of them returned to Asia. Maintaining their numbers depended heavily on continued immigration. The resentment their presence aroused reflected racism, but other factors were definitely involved. The British-Canadian majority wanted BC to be British and English-Canadian. Those who assimilated easily were welcome, like Germans, Americans or Scandinavians. Those who might not assimilate easily were discriminated against, including Natives, Chinese, Japanese, and East Indians. But Italians and eastern Europeans were also discriminated against. Rich English-Canadians welcomed Asian immigrants to work in their homes and businesses; working-class English-Canadians resented them because they lowered wages. Such prejudices were nationalist, religious, and class, as well as racial.

The Native population stabilized at around 20,000, accounting for 25% of the province in 1891, 10% in 1901, and only 5% by 1911. The failure of the federal government to negotiate treaties left their legal status in limbo, and they could not vote. Less than five percent of BC is arable, and the provincial government took more and more land from the natives and gave it to white settlers or businesses. When railways were built, whites were compensated for the loss of land, Natives were not. Many natives sought jobs in the white economy where they worked in fishing, forestry, agriculture and a host of activities. They were usually seasonal workers, going back to their villages in the winter to hunt and trap.

Gradually many of the Natives were converted to various Christian denominations, but that supplemented rather than replaced their ancient culture and beliefs. Poverty, neglect, discrimination and the ravages of white man's diseases continued to affect them. While the provincial government provided adequate education facilities for the enormous white population, the federal government provided little funding for the small Native community. A survey done in 1921 revealed that one-third of Natives did not speak English and 40% of children over ten were illiterate. The governments continued the campaign to wipe out the culture of potlatches, paradoxically making it illegal for Natives to give wooden carvings to each other, and then seizing these wonderful artifacts and giving them to the government's museums and hence to the white population. A century later some of those artifacts were returned to the Natives.

From the time of the gold rush a few people from continental Europe had added to the ethnic mix of BC. More came to help build the railways, and even more to work the mines and smelters. Almost all major European ethnic groups were represented – Germans, Scandinavians, Slavs, Jews, Italians – but unlike the prairies, BC did not become home to huge settlements of continental Europeans, a fact which enhanced its British character. Almost no French Canadians migrated that far west, and most that did were soon assimilated. An exception to this limited European migration was the Doukhobors. In 1912 their visionary leader, Peter Veregin, led 5,000 of them to Castlegar and Grand Forks. There they bought huge tracks of land where they shared residences and dining halls and worked together on community-owned land. They refused to provide the government with vital statistics or to send their children to public schools, regarding both as a violation of their religious beliefs.

These were the 250,000 British Columbians whom Premier McBride came to govern. To broaden his government's base he gained the support of the two Socialist MLAs by passing legislation to reduce hours of work and improve safety conditions in mining. To deal with a crisis in the province's finances he introduced strict economies while carrying on the policy of leasing vast tracts of forest at low prices. Although much of the province's timber land was leased to private companies, the revenues helped balance the budget by 1905. He then launched a major program of public works and railway construction to sustain and support the economic boom, open up new regions, attract investment, and keep pace with the exploding population.

McBride dusted off the old cry that Ottawa owed BC "better terms". He demanded higher subsidies and stormed out of a meeting when Ottawa did not meet his demands. Arguing that BC needed a strong government to defend the province's interests, he called an election after only three years in office, and won 26 of 42 seats, leaving the Liberals 13 and the Socialists three. Finally BC had a government based on a single political party, with broad political support based on a province-wide organization, on both the island and the mainland, and from both industry and labour.

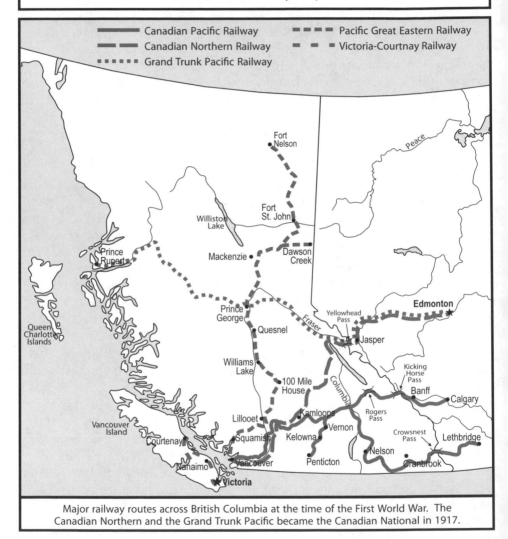

British Columbia Railways Map

Major railway routes across British Columbia at the time of the First World War. The Canadian Northern and the Grand Trunk Pacific became the Canadian National in 1917.

McBride continued to attract the support of both rich capitalists and the working man. More subsidies were handed out to railways, in particular to assist the Canadian Northern to build a line from Edmonton over the Yellowhead Pass to Kamloops. It would then run beside the CPR all the way to Vancouver, costing millions and providing no additional service to the province. Both the Minister of Finance and the Minister of Lands resigned in protest over the waste. The Canadian Northern received so much in subsidies that it used part of the surplus to purchase the Dominion Coal Company. McBride provided generous subsidies to another railway in the Kootenays without even discussing them with Cabinet. Swept up in the mindless optimism, the public endorsed the wild spending in the election of 1909, increasing McBride's majority to 38, and leaving only two Liberals and two Socialists to question the government's actions.

For McBride, the winning formula meant more of the same. New labour and health benefits were the best in Canada. New subsidies brought more railway construction. The northern half of the province had scarcely been touched by development, so subsidies were approved for the Grand Trunk Railway to build a line from Edmonton to Prince Rupert. Another railway, the Pacific Great Eastern (PGE), was to cross the province from North Vancouver to the northeast, through Prince George and eventually up to the Peace River country. In 1911 a four-day session of the Assembly produced massive grants for these and two other railways to open up more regions of the province. Continued prosperity rained down on the province. A triumphal visit to London produced favourable publicity from high-level meetings, banquets, and a five-hour audience with the King. Back in BC McBride easily won the 1912 election, increasing the Conservative majority to 40. Now the opposition consisted of the two lonely Socialists.

Then in 1913 Glad-Hand Dick's luck started to run out. The economic boom that he had personified came to an end. Investment declined and unemployment rose. The railways that the province had so lavishly subsidized were not finished or were not producing revenue. The bonds that the province had guaranteed, and which had paid for the construction, were, however, coming due for payment. There had always been considerable labour unrest and strike action, but it mounted as companies tried to maintain profits by cutting wages. McBride's gestures to the working man, such as shorter work days and better work conditions, had always been more political than they were meaningful, and labour was growing tired of mere sops. Rumours of corruption had always been an element in politics and gossip, and the strange and quick way railway charters were approved provided much grist for the newspapers. McBride had ignored mounting demands for reform, particularly the allied movements of women's suffrage and prohibition. His province did not even have a proper university, though some land had been bought west of Vancouver and an affiliate of McGill provided university courses and degrees. He had spent so much time enjoying London's high society that he had become something of an absentee landlord in his fiefdom of British Columbia. Fortunately for Dick McBride the outbreak of World War I would give him a new role as one of Canada's great patriots.

Chapter Seven

The Great War and the Troubled Twenties, 1914-1929

Canada was automatically at war when Great Britain declared war on Germany on 4 August 1914. Three days earlier Premier Richard McBride took a decisive step to assist the war effort. Two submarines were sitting in the Seattle dockyards, just built for the Chilean navy but not yet paid for. Without any authority, McBride bought them and ordered them to sail to Esquimalt. They arrived the day Canada went to war. A grateful federal government immediately bought them, but for five days BC had its own navy.

McBride's determination to help the mother country was shared across the province. Tens of thousands of men volunteered immediately. By war's end, 55,000 had enlisted, an amazing 10% of the population and an extremely high percentage of the adult males, the highest enlistment rate in Canada and 20% higher than Ontario's. The rate reflected the high proportion of British-born, the British character of the province, the higher proportion of single men, and high unemployment. The first shipload left in August including a Vancouver business-man, Arthur Currie, who eventually commanded all of Canada's soldiers and led the troops who stormed Vimy Ridge in 1917. Six thousand of those men died and another 13,000 were wounded. Such was their bravery that thirteen returned with the Victoria Cross, the Empire's highest decoration. The absence of so many young men severely affected social and economic life, as women and children attempted to fill the void left in their lives and communities.

The west coast was almost completely unprepared for war. German naval vessels were in the Pacific, capable of attacking ships and cities, and apart from the two new submarines, Canada had but a few old guns at Esquimalt, a small supply of ammunition, and one old gunship. Improvements were made, but fortunately the German warships found other targets before they were swept from the seas.

The absence of fortifications had, however, a profound effect on the population. British Columbians worried that German forces would land and combine with the local German immigrant population to occupy part of the province. In fact, there was no such threat and the fear reflected the hysteria born of isolation and wild imagination. Nevertheless, pressure grew to lock up the province's tiny German minority. When a German submarine sank the passenger liner *Lusitania* in 1915, a rumour spread that some Germans had celebrated the event. That sparked a riot in Vancouver in which German shops were torched. Eventually most of the potential "enemy aliens" were imprisoned in camps around the province.

The war deepened the economic recession. As money was diverted to the war effort, the demand and the price for exports like minerals and fresh fruit declined. The war effectively ended investment in the province. Immigration dried up as did revenue from land sales. Construction of housing, buildings and railways slowed dramatically, and unemployment increased. Ottawa chose to produce the equipment for war from the factories of Central Canada, and they sought BC inputs only after eastern Canadian mines, lumber camps and factories were running at capacity. As revenue declined and unemployment and welfare costs grew, the province's financial situation worsened.

The provincial government had to borrow money to pay interest on the bonds and subsidies lavished on excessive railway construction. By 1915 revenue was half the 1912 level. The decision to support three additional railways across the province – the Grand Trunk Pacific, the Canadian Northern and the PGE – helped contribute to construction and duplication that greatly exceeded the province's needs or finances. The first two railroads went bankrupt and were nationalized by the federal government to form the Canadian National (CNR). But Ottawa refused to take over the PGE, which remained a huge drain on BC's finances for decades.

McBride had long left the detailed administration of government to his able Finance Minister, William Bowser, and now he became even more of a figurehead. He spent more time in London, seemingly less and less interested in the premiership. When he did return to Victoria, he pressed for more subsidies for the PGE. Bowser and a growing number of MLAs disagreed, and McBride's influence declined further. In December, 1915, he resigned, dying of ill-health less than two years later, still in his mid-fifties.

McBride and Bowser had been a formidable team because Bowser had qualities McBride lacked, namely ruthlessness, decisiveness, and attention to detail. Premier Bowser quickly developed a reform program to deal with growing problems like corruption. The people were not convinced because the Conservatives had been ignoring those issues for years. The Conservative's massive spending on railways had not yet paid off, and no trains were running on the PGE. The smell of corruption was in the air, and one Minister was forced to resign for buying horses at an advantageous price from a government agency.

The Liberals acquired a new leader in the hard-working and honest Harlan Brewster. They adopted a reform program that promised action on the two main political issues of the day, women's suffrage and prohibition, and on a host of other economic and social issues. In the 1916 election, Brewster and his Liberals swept to power with 37 seats. The Conservatives dropped from

40 to ten. The Liberals launched a reform blitz, including the creation of the first Department of Labour in Canada, extension of the eight-hour day to more sectors of the economy, better worker's compensation, mother's pensions, a Minimum Wages Act and minimum wages for women, better health and education, efforts to regulate utilities, and attempts to ensure the province received more direct benefits from the forest industry. It also included women's suffrage, which had been approved 2:1 in the last all-male election. Mary Ellen Smith was elected in 1920 and became the first female Cabinet Minister in the British Commonwealth.

Brewster genuinely wanted to provide honest and reformist government, but he fell short of the goal. He set up a number of commissions to look into corruption. The goal, of course, was to find Conservative wrongdoings. One commission duly found that the PGE had received subsidies without any inspection of construction, and the Conservatives apparently received favours in return. The Liberals adopted a series of measures to reduce such irregularities in government finances. They also got caught in their own clean-up campaign when the new Attorney General had to resign for accepting campaign funds from the CNR.

Brewster's biggest political problem was the demand by the Temperance League for the abolition of liquor. A majority had voted for it in the referendum, and it became illegal to sell or drink alcohol in public places. It was not, however, illegal to drink it at home, to manufacture it for export, or to use it for medicinal purposes. Those loopholes meant that companies were soon making fortunes smuggling legal alcohol into the USA, some of which re-appeared in BC. Bootleggers were soon making vast quantities of illegal alcohol for private consumption; and doctors were besieged by formerly healthy citizens whose ills could only be cured by brandy. Doctors signed almost 200,000 prescriptions for alcohol in 1919, and one doctor treated 4,000 needy patients in a single month. Brewster thought that W.C. Finlay, Secretary of the People's Prohibition Party, would be the perfect choice for Liquor Commissioner, but Finlay illegally imported hundreds of cases of liquor and went to jail instead.

In the meantime, the war-time demands for ammunition and equipment had finally produced a boom in the mines and forests. A shortage of labour developed in 1916 because of the boom, the heavy enlistment in the services, the imprisonment of aliens and the return of Chinese and Japanese to Asia. Women started entering the work force in large numbers. Wages rose, but prices rose much faster – 30% in 1917 - and the working class found its standard of living in sharp decline. Membership in unions soared, and strikes became more frequent, bitter and long. From 1917 to 1919 there were dozens of strikes in mining, transportation and industry. Basically they failed because of ruthless owners, patriotism, government support for the owners, divisions within the labour movement over politics and policies, and the fact that many workers did not want to be unionized.

As the war dragged on, it became increasingly difficult for Canada to maintain its army at full strength. The federal government came under intense pressure to conscript men for the army. Many disagreed, particularly when government was doing little to control prices, and huge profits were being reaped by those who owned factories and mines. Workers demanded that if labour was going to be conscripted, then wealth should be conscripted as well, an idea the government refused to entertain. When conscription was adopted, some workers fled into the forests. One worker, Albert Goodwin, was captured and died while in custody. When a secret enquiry found no evidence of wrongdoing by the police, his fellow workers went on strike.

In March 1918 Brewster became the fourth BC premier to die in office, the victim of pneumonia. His Cabinet was so loaded with talented competitors that it took four ballots for John Oliver to emerge as the new leader. The son of a coal miner, Oliver was a self-made, self-educated high-school drop-out who had worked in construction, forests, and mines. He had become a successful farmer, and had little sympathy for those who couldn't make it on their own sweat or resorted to strike action to get a better salary. But "Honest John, the Farmer's Friend" stayed in inexpensive hotels, ate in ordinary restaurants, and travelled to Ottawa on a regular ticket. He immediately set to work to improve the province's financial situation, stimulate the economy, solve the PGE's problems and prepare for the end of the war.

Oliver's greatest challenge was finding work for returning veterans. Almost 10% of the population had enlisted, a huge proportion of the adult male population. Their jobs had been taken by foreigners, women, the physically unfit, and the less patriotic. They could not simply be dismissed to make way for returning soldiers. Because of the warm climate, veterans from other parts of Canada chose to be demobilized in BC. Many veterans were scarred physically and mentally by the war, which made work more of a challenge. But as the wartime boom ended, factories and mines were laying off employees, not expanding.

Oliver's main answer was to help the veterans become farmers, a good, honest and healthy lifestyle in his opinion. But few veterans pined for the rural lifestyle. In short, there was no short-term solution for unemployed soldiers, and they became another element of discontent in a rapidly deteriorating labour situation. Strikes multiplied as companies reduced wages. Soldiers were hired as scabs or thugs to break the strikes; hardly the hero's welcome in the better world they had spent four years fighting for in the trenches of the Western Front. In May 1919 a twenty-five day strike began in support of the Winnipeg General Strike, just one of many serious and violent strikes at war's end.

War changed the population of BC. It became less British because so many British-born volunteered for service, and many of them were killed or didn't return. It became more Canadian as pride in Canadian achievement displaced British patriotism and Canada moved towards nationhood and independence. Many Orientals went back to Asia during the recession of 1913-15. The war changed attitudes as people became less tolerant of foreigners, more willing to use political clout to force values like prohibition on others, and more willing to use strikes and violence to protest exploitation.

Premier Oliver worked to diversify the economy, especially developing agriculture by irrigating dry lands, draining marshes, opening the Peace River country, and getting veterans to settle on the land. The PGE continued to absorb subsidies rapidly and progress slowly. Oliver finally expropriated it and completed the section from Squamish to Quesnel. Some trains actually began running, but the railway lost money. The ill-fated railway finally chugged into Dawson Creek in 1931, but the Depression then forestalled the economic development the PGE was designed to facilitate. The government then shifted the emphasis on infrastructure from railways to roads. In 1927 the first gravel highway was completed through the mountains linking Vancouver to the prairies.

Oliver tried to present the Liberals as the party of reform, but their record was checkered at best. In the 1916 election they had championed civil service reform and hiring on merit. Unfortunately, Liberal supporters who had worked for the party for years now believed they were entitled to their reward in the form of government contracts and jobs. That is how the system had always worked, and civil service reform waited while hundreds of Liberals replaced Conservatives in the administration and as the contractors for government work and services. Oliver struggled with the impossibility of enforcing prohibition, and finally allowed the sale of liquor in government stores. A further retreat allowed the sale of beer by the glass, to white men only, and only in licensed premises. Licenses then went to those with good Liberal connections, and prohibition began corrupting politicians as well as police and judges.

With a mixed record of dealing with reform, the returned veterans and labour unrest, Oliver faced the electorate in 1920. The Liberals lost 11 seats winning only 26 while the Conservatives picked up five seats for a total of 15. Discontent with both parties was reflected in the election of four Labour candidates and three Independents, the decision of some Liberal MLAs to sit as independents, and the formation of a new Provincial Party. An aspect of reform that did not appeal to the Liberals was the concept of one-man-one vote. In rural constituencies a few voters elected many Liberals while in urban areas huge electorates elected a few Socialists, and Vancouver remained underrepresented in Cabinet.

With the Liberals failing to deal with the province's problems, the Conservatives seemingly incapable of promoting alternate solutions, and the Socialists garnering little support outside the cities, the province was ripe for a new political movement. Similar conditions across Canada had produced farmers' governments in Ontario, Manitoba, and Alberta, as well as a new Progressive Party with the second largest number of seat in the House of Commons. Into the vacuum rushed Colonel A.D. McRae, a rich and confident member of the elite whose leadership qualities had been proven in battle. He rallied the rich businessmen, farmers, and veterans, all of whom felt neglected by the government.

The Liberals went into the 1924 election in worse shape than in 1920. The economy had rebounded, but their record of managing problems remained mixed. The Conservatives were still divided, but even under the unpopular Bowser they were gaining support as a result of the Liberal decline. When the votes were counted, McRae and his Provincial Party had taken 24% of the ballots but only three seats. The Conservatives had taken 30% of the vote, which gave them 17 seats. The Liberals took 31% and 23 seats, and they now needed the support of the Socialists to govern.

The 1920s presented a mixed picture economically. The recession that immediately followed the war gradually eased. The labour unrest and strikes that dominated the headlines from 1917 to 1919 ended with victory for the industrialists and a serious weakening of the labour unions. The 1920s then saw considerable growth in the economy, but it was uneven and precarious. It was a period of rapid technological advance. The relative price of cars declined, and car ownership jumped from 15,000 to 100,000. That produced a social revolution, as many people could travel considerable distances for the first time, could travel as families, and young couples could escape the close chaperoning of their parents. Mining, fishing, forestry and construction all boomed, and British Columbians enjoyed the highest per capita income in Canada, some 15% above their nearest rival in Ontario. It was also the fastest growing province in Canada, its population increasing from 525,000 in 1921 to 700,000 in 1931, almost twice the national rate of growth.

This apparent prosperity, however, masked serious structural flaws related to geography and the way the federal government had designed the post-Confederation Canadian economy. One aspect of that policy, known as the "National Policy" and of the regulations that implemented it, was that freight rates seriously harmed BC's economic prospects. One example was that it cost as much to ship Alberta wheat 1200 kilometers to the Lakehead as it did to ship it 800 kilometers to Vancouver, so Central Canada handled one of the nation's largest exports.

Premier Oliver launched a campaign for "better terms" to deal with discriminatory freight and tariff rates, the great distance from BC to Central Canada, and the mountainous terrain which made transportation abnormally expensive in BC. He also demanded the return of land given to Ottawa to subsidize the building of the CPR. Even if his demands failed, it was good politics to attack the federal government, the eastern financial interests and of course the CPR. Oliver achieved some success: freight rates across the Rockies were cut 50%, and grain exports through Vancouver jumped from 4% of Canada's exports in 1920 to 40% in 1932.

Throughout the twenties the Liberals continued their slow decline, kept in office mainly by massive over-representation of the rural regions. In 1926 Oliver was diagnosed with cancer. He offered to retire, but was so popular that the Liberals insisted he remain premier, and he became the fifth BC premier to die in office. He was replaced by the lackluster John McLean. He could not arrest the party's decline or find new vision and new ideas. Problems went unsolved, charges of corruption filled the air, both Vancouver and Victoria fretted with their lack of representation in government, and internal dissention wracked the party as it drifted towards defeat.

The Conservatives finally replaced Bowser with Dr. Simon Fraser Tolmie, a charming and popular veterinarian who had been an MP since 1917. He had proven credentials as federal Minister of Agriculture, and was not linked to the bitter disputes within the party. Tolmie had deep roots in the province, being the son of a fur trader and a Metis woman. The 1928 election was basically a personality contest which brought the Conservatives a gain of 20 seats to 35 and the Liberals a loss of 11 for 12 seats. Tolmie appointed a good Cabinet with representation from Vancouver. In normal times it should have been able to breathe some new life into government and continue with the province's development. But much more than that would be needed when the great Depression struck in 1929.

Chapter Eight

The Great Depression, 1930-1939

The great Depression of the 1930s was a national and global catastrophe, and it hit BC with devastating effect. The cycle of economic "boom and bust" had gone on for centuries, with periods of high economic activity and increasing prosperity followed by periods of stagnation, falling income, and poverty for many. There had been recessions in the 1860s, the 1890s, and before and after World War I, each then followed by good times.

The recession that began in 1929 with the collapse of the New York stock market quickly became much worse than previous ones. Countries sought to protect domestic industry by raising tariffs to exclude foreign goods. The policy failed. Exports from all countries declined, the relative cost of goods increased, and factories laid off workers. Banks called in their loans and made it very difficult for companies or people to borrow. Investment almost ceased, and with it the jobs and the demand for goods that investment created. There was an immediate decline in the amount of money in circulation. People became more frugal, so the demand for goods declined even more. Factories laid off even more workers in a downward spiral of decreasing economic activity, rising unemployment and increasing poverty.

This happened everywhere in Canada. Within a few years the demand for BC minerals had fallen by 50% and the demand for its fish and forest products by 65%. BC exports declined 60% between 1929 and 1934. Soon 67,000 people were unemployed, and by 1933 it was 100,000, one person in seven in the entire population. The Depression was worse on the prairies and in the Maritimes, but BC faced a problem unique to Canadian provinces. Because of the favourable climate, tens of thousands of unemployed from other provinces flooded in, placing an intolerable burden on welfare, which was a municipal and provincial responsibility. The unemployment rate reached 28% in 1933, the highest in Canada, while provincial revenue declined almost 25%.

The problems of welfare, unemployment, and rural people flooding into the towns and cities soon overwhelmed municipal governments, especially Vancouver. Declining property taxes, a narrow tax base and fixed payments on previous debts left municipalities incapable of coping with the rising demand for welfare. Indeed, they often cut expenditures to save money, putting even more people out of work. As poverty and hopelessness radicalized the unemployed, they turned to ideologies like Communism. This led the well-to-do and the employed to view the poor as threatening, making those in power more willing to use violence to control demonstrations rather than seek solutions to the Depression itself.

The Tolmie government was not prepared to deal with the Depression politically, ideologically or financially. Tolmie and his Cabinet had no ideas for fighting the Depression, a lack of imagination shared by every other government in Canada, as well as the main opposition parties. Like those governments, Tolmie also lacked the will or initiative to look for new ways to deal with the magnitude of the problem. The conventional financial wisdom of the day was that governments should balance their budgets. When revenue fell, Tolmie cut expenditures, increased taxes and downloaded hospitalization and mother's pensions on the municipalities. Business, the one sector of the population that might have supported Tolmie, regarded the cuts as completely inadequate.

These measures made conditions worse. The cuts in spending added to unemployment, and the unemployed spent less, further reducing the demand for goods and services. The tax increases took money out of people's pockets which reduced demand even more. In the first few years of the Depression unemployed men created huge "hobo jungles" or camps along railway lines, under bridges, or near the waterfront. Vancouver was soon host to an overwhelming number of people on welfare. To get the unemployed out of the cities the government put 18,000 men in 237 work camps, where they got board and room and 20 cents a day in return for hard labour building public works. Soon the province could not afford them, and the federal Department of Defence took over. It introduced strict military discipline, virtually turning the camps into prisons and needlessly increasing discontent, anger and bitterness.

While the Conservative government struggled with the Depression, the Liberals were rejuvenated under the leadership of Duff Pattullo. He was one of the bright and able politicians who had swept to power in 1917, and had held the key portfolio of Lands for 12 years. He was outgoing, bold, decisive, expensively dressed, and a good speaker. He was a pragmatist, always looking for ideas. He toured the province and listened to the people. Then he appointed a committee of experts to put together a wide-ranging platform calling for massive public works, better schools and hospitals and lower freight rates.

By the time an election was called on 2 November 1933 it was clear that the Conservatives would lose heavily but less clear who would win. Pattullo and the Liberals had a slogan "work and wages" and a good platform that emphasized ending unemployment through public works. But the 1930s saw the emergence of a viable socialist party, the Co-operative Commonwealth Federation, or CCF. Socialist parties had been winning seats in BC provincial and municipal elections for decades. At a convention in Calgary in 1932, socialists from across Canada joined with labour, academic radicals and agrarian populists to form the CCF, which soon became a major party at the federal level and in all provinces west of Quebec.

The CCF believed that the Depression resulted from fundamental flaws in the capitalist system, and that only radical change could restore prosperity, produce growth and create equality. They advocated the nationalization of resource industries and banking, a major expansion of health, education and welfare services, and shifting the tax burden to the wealthy. In the election, the CCF captured a third of the vote and seven seats to become the official opposition. The Liberals formed the government with 34 seats, and the Conservatives completely disappeared.

Premier Pattullo immediately set out to deal with the Depression as best he could, given the province's financial situation and constitutional limitations. He launched a road-building program, increased spending on education, increased funding for municipalities, reduced taxes on the poorest, gave assistance to mining and fishing, and made it harder for banks to foreclose on mortgages. Unlike Tolmie, he was willing to borrow millions of dollars to fund needed programs.

Pattullo understood, however, that only the federal government had the tools necessary to deal with the Depression, namely large financial resources and control of monetary policy, banking and currency. He was a supporter of American President Franklin Roosevelt, who believed that the solution lay with massive government spending based on heavy borrowing, a theory known as Keynesian economics. Pattullo had read widely, and with an open mind. He was clearly a Keynesian, and as such was years ahead of contemporary politicians, especially the federal Conservatives and Liberals. Pattullo also toyed with the idea of having the government create credit or purchasing power, a concept he called "socialized credit". This was what the Social Credit party was advocating in Alberta, but it was within federal jurisdiction and the federal government did not accept this significant change to monetary policy until World War II.

Premier Pattullo was correct to believe that only the federal government had the resources to finance huge spending on public works. The problem was that the Conservative government in Ottawa was unwilling to do so. It did provide some assistance, but it usually insisted on a voice in how the money was spent. To Pattulo that meant an unacceptable loss of provincial independence, and he refused money on those terms. In 1935 he launched a radio campaign to press the federal government to do more for BC. He attended federal-provincial conferences, arguing that BC had become home to one-third of Canada's unemployed, and the whole nation should be supporting them through federal grants.

He wanted the federal government to set up a national unemployment plan, pay the interest on provincial debt, reduce tariff and freight rates and take over the Pacific Great Eastern Railway but his pleas fell on deaf ears.

The Liberal programs helped thousands of people, but hardly made a dint in an unemployment rate of 30% and in the suffering of hundreds of thousands of people. In April 1935 1,700 men marched from the relief camps to Vancouver to demand work. Their demonstrations were peaceful, but the mayor read the Riot Act, giving the police extra power just in case. For a while they occupied the Hudson's Bay store. The federal government refused to talk to them, and after two months they began the famous "On-to-Ottawa Trek" to take their concerns directly to the national government. Their numbers grew to 2,500 along the way, and ordinary people in every town gave them food. That march was violently broken up in Regina, whose mayor talked the men into hopping freight cars back to BC.

Pattullo grew increasingly frustrated as the policies and spending he had initiated failed to affect unemployment rates and the public and press grew increasingly critical of his failure. Once more there was talk of secession from Canada. His relations with the press deteriorated, and he used radio increasingly to communicate directly with the public. His relations with Ottawa also deteriorated as he attacked the federal government for failing to address the Depression or BC's unique situation. In effect, he needed federal money to implement his programs and policies, and he could not convince them to adopt those policies. He pushed for the construction of a new bridge over the Fraser River at New Westminster, a project that would cost four times the annual highways department budget. He forced his Cabinet to accept it, but five Liberal MLAs voted against it, foreshadowing increasing problems within the party.

By 1937 an election was looming and Pattullo's Liberal government was in danger of defeat. Fortunately for them, the Conservatives were still seriously divided although they were picking up considerable support from their traditional base, the business community and disillusioned Liberals. The CCF was also seriously divided. The purist faction wanted to promise radical change to the capitalist system; the pragmatists wanted a more moderate platform that would attract more voters and less criticism. The purists won the debate and the CCF entered the election with a radical program, serious internal divisions and a new leader. As a result, the CCF may have lost an election it could have won. The Liberals took 37% of the vote which ensured their re-election with 31 seats. The Conservatives regained their position as official opposition with eight seats, and the CCF fell to third place with seven seats.

Pattullo's dreams for a massive program of public works faded for lack of provincial revenue. He enunciated a northern vision for the development of the Peace River country and the annexation of the Yukon, something few people in the Yukon wanted. He carried on his fights with Ottawa, but without success. Pattullo suspected that the federal government wanted to transfer power permanently from the provincial to the federal level, and he became an increasingly rigid defender of provincial rights. The federal Liberal government of Mackenzie King had launched a massive study of the functioning of federalism known as the Rowell-Sirois Commission. The BC submission defended provincial rights, but the other parties disagreed with Pattullo's position. The report did recommend the transfer of power to Ottawa, so Pattullo joined the premiers of Ontario and Alberta in rejecting it.

In order to fight Ottawa, Pattullo passed a law to give his Cabinet more power. Many people thought it unnecessary, and it added to his reputation for authoritarianism without actually yielding benefit in the battles with Ottawa. To protect consumers he tried to fix maximum and minimum prices for coal and petroleum. The gasoline companies refused to sell gas at the lower price, and the courts ruled that the price controls were unconstitutional. He also tried to regulate the prices of utilities like electricity, telegraph and transportation. These projects were piecemeal, not part of any overall strategy, so they annoyed the business community without seriously undermining support for the CCF. Pattullo had also tried to introduce health insurance before the election, but it had proved so divisive an issue that he shelved it for five years.

Faced with the continued arrival of unemployed men from other provinces, Pattullo announced that there would be no assistance to outsiders. He also reduced support for the municipalities. The federal government closed the relief camps, putting even more unemployed in the cities, and Vancouver banned begging, the main source of food for the men. In June, 1938, an angry crowd marched on and then occupied three Vancouver landmarks, the Art Gallery, the General Post Office and the Hotel Georgia. They soon left the Hotel Georgia, but they stayed in the Post Office for six weeks, and were finally forced out by tear gas fired by the RCMP. After that they rioted down Hastings and Granville Streets breaking windows. Another big demonstration soon followed at the police station where large crowds demanded the release of those arrested for rioting.

Premier Pattullo blamed Ottawa for the demonstrations. Conservatives and Liberals blamed the CCF. The CCF blamed the provincial Liberal government and called for an election. Business became increasingly worried about the radicalization of the unemployed, the growing popularity of the CCF and Pattullo's failure to handle the situation or to obtain cooperation and assistance from Ottawa. Their conclusion was that only a coalition of Liberals and Conservatives could prevent the CCF from winning the next election. But BC and Canada were about to trade one nightmare for another. The horrors of another European War would soon put an end to the woes of the decade-long Depression.

Chapter Nine

World War II and the Post-War Boom, 1945-1952

World War II brought an end to the Depression in BC. Shortly after war was declared, Ottawa began spending hundreds of millions of dollars on recruiting, equipping and housing the rapidly growing armed forces. Some of the spending was financed by creating money through the Bank of Canada, which the federal government was willing to do to fight a war but had not done to fight the Depression. Unlike in World War I, a sizeable portion of federal spending went to BC from the beginning of the war, and employment quickly expanded in forestry, mining, fishing and agriculture, shipbuilding and aircraft manufacture.

Canada had become fully independent from Britain with the signing of the Statute of Westminster on 11 November 1931, and it waited for one week after Britain went to war in order to affirm that independence. But pro-British sentiment remained strong, and once more a greater proportion of British Columbians volunteered than elsewhere in Canada. In all, 90,000 or 10% of the population went to war, but the number killed was less than half the rate as in the first war.

Premier Pattullo's fortunes, however, continued to decline. He had identified himself very strongly with provincial rights, but in wartime most people wanted a stronger central government. Many Liberals and Conservatives and businessmen believed that only a united Liberal-Conservative coalition could keep the CCF out of power. Pattullo strongly disagreed, but he lost the argument, and resigned. His able Minister of Finance, John Hart, became premier. In the ensuing election the Liberals won 21 seats which they combined with 12 Conservative seats for a strong majority of 33. The CCF collected the most votes at over 33%, but that translated into only 14 seats.

As in World War I, isolation bred hysteria, the worry now being the presence of 23,000 Japanese-Canadians, most born in Canada. They did not support nor sympathize with Japan, and the police judged that they were not a threat. They were, however, concentrated in the fishing industry, and people worried that they might smuggle Japanese soldiers into the country. On 7 December 1941 Japan attacked the American Pacific fleet at Pearl Harbour in Hawaii. Within months the Japanese had overrun Hong Kong, killing or capturing 600 Canadian soldiers, overran Singapore, occupied several of Alaska's Aleutian Islands, and even fired a few shells harmlessly at the BC coast.

Many people and the provincial government demanded that the Japanese be removed from the coast. Beginning in February 1942, they were moved inland, women and children to abandoned mining towns, many of the men to jobs on the prairies. Their boats, farms and property were seized and sold, often for low prices, a clear manifestation of the jealousy and racism that also underlay the removal. At the end of the war the federal government gave them a choice of moving to any province east of BC or to Japan – many of them refused, and they were eventually allowed to return to the coast. Forty years later they were given compensation for the property that had been, in effect, stolen from them. In 1949 they were finally given the vote.

By 1940 production was back to the levels of 1929 and by 1945 output had doubled. Throughout the war the BC economy boomed with the enormous demand for all the products it had traditionally produced, plus the new manufactured goods demanded by the war. When the United States decided to build a secure highway to protect Alaska, part of it ran from Dawson Creek to Watson Lake in the Yukon, finally opening up the northeastern corner of the province. A highway was built from Peace River to Prince Rupert, whose population doubled during the war. The PGE finally reached Dawson Creek setting a railway record for being late, in this case, by over 30 years. The northeast joined the economic boom, Dawson Creek growing from a village of 500 to a town of 4,500 in 1942.

In the Second World War the federal government controlled inflation, so the economy was not plagued by strikes. Wages were high, goods were scarce and people were encouraged to buy bonds to pay for the war effort. That reduced personal consumption and freed up goods for the wartime effort. It also left the population with large savings and pent-up demand for all the things they had gone without since the Depression struck in 1929. In 1945 personal demand replaced the war's demand, the factories switched from making tanks and artillery to making cars and refrigerators, and the good times roared on. After the war the rapid economic expansion provided good employment for the returning veterans, and many of the women who had replaced men in factories and business remained in the work force.

The post-war spending spree produced a social revolution. Trucks replaced horses on the farm and in transportation. Rural electrification changed life on the farm. Cars were readily available for the first time, making travel faster, easier and cheaper for both business and pleasure. Drive-in movies appeared, TVs became available, and dances and homemade music declined in popularity. A simple technological innovation like the chain saw revolutionized the lives of thousands of forestry workers. The refrigerator, vacuum cleaner and washing machine greatly reduced household drudgery. More women entered the work force, which changed family life, and their additional spending power added even more to the economic boom. More people moved to the towns and cities, and BC became the most urbanized province in Canada. Technology and union pressure produced a shorter work week, but part of that saving was then consumed by commuting time as cities spread into the suburbs. From 1931 to 1941 the population increased by a third, to 1,165,000. Vancouver grew to 300,000, becoming the third largest city in Canada.

The economy also changed in significant ways. It became more diversified, with the development of dams, electricity, manufacturing, pipelines to bring oil from Alberta, and more processing of raw materials before export. In 1951-52 Alcan diverted an entire river to produce electricity for an aluminum smelter. It was the largest construction site in the world, and a new city of Kitimat was created with a population of 13,500. There was massive consolidation in industry as a few giant companies bought out the smaller ones. The number of fish canning companies, for example, fell from almost one hundred before World War I to sixteen after World War II. Five companies came to dominate the forestry industry.

As the boom continued, immigration once more met the demand for labour. As usual, large numbers came from the rest of Canada, Great Britain and central and northern Europe. Large numbers of unskilled labour came from Italy, Portugal and Greece, and immigration resumed from Asia, especially from China and India. This new wave of Asian immigration did not produce the backlash of white racism previously experienced. The discovery of the horrors of racism in the concentration camps of Nazi Europe brought reflection on the treatment of the Japanese during the war and of the Chinese since the 1860s. By 1949 the Natives, Chinese, Japanese, and East Indians were all allowed to vote. That recognition of full citizenship also meant they could enter professions like law and politics. Racial discrimination did not, however, disappear, particularly regarding the treatment of Natives whose population and prospects had stagnated since the late nineteenth century.

Riding the wave of prosperity was the Coalition Government. The main goal of the government was to keep the CCF out of power. Having achieved that by winning the 1941 election, it settled in to administer the province until the next election. Basically its policy was "more of the same" in terms of building roads, schools, and hospitals for the expanding population and economy. It did, however, achieve some important modernization, as with the consolidation of over 600 school districts into less than 100. The one-room school house became a thing of nostalgia and students moved to larger and better-equipped schools.

In 1945 the Coalition called an election to take advantage of the euphoria of victory, the return of the troops, labour peace, prosperity, full employment, and a bright future. Premier Hart had provided competent administration, and the provincial and federal governments had avoided the mistakes that had added so much to the suffering of World War I. The Coalition lost five percent of the vote but actually gained four seats for a solid majority of 37. The CCF increased its vote share to 37% but only won 10 seats. John Hart resigned in 1947, replaced by the dull and uninspiring Bryon "Boss" Johnson. The 1949 election vindicated coalition politics once again, with the Coalition increasing its vote share and gaining two more seats, while CCF strength fell to seven.

After the election, both coalition partners began to resent sharing the spoils of office, and both thought they could win an election on their own. The Conservatives in particular grew discontented with the deal that gave the Liberals the position of premier in perpetuity so they decided to destroy the coalition. As Minister of Finance their leader, Herbert Anscomb, had negotiated a new deal with Ottawa. He announced it at a press conference, putting the premier and other cabinet ministers in the untenable position of learning what their government was doing from the newspapers.

The premier immediately demanded Anscomb's resignation, and he and the other ten Conservatives left the Coalition to replace the CCF as the official opposition. In a bizarre twist, Premier Johnson said that he had only demanded the resignation of Anscomb, so the Coalition was still in effect. When the Assembly met in February 1952 the CCF moved a motion of non-confidence in the Liberal minority government. In another bizarre twist, the Conservatives supported the Liberals, proving that the Coalition was indeed still in effect. Then Premier Johnson called an election for June 12.

The 1952 election was one of the most bizarre in Canadian history, and one of the most important in BC history. The main goal of both Liberals and Conservatives was still to keep the CCF from forming a government. To achieve this they now adopted the transferable ballot. By this system of voting, a candidate had to win over 50% of votes to be elected. To determine that, every elector rated the candidates in his constituency from first to last. If no one had a majority on the first count, then the candidate with the fewest votes was eliminated. The second choices of those who had voted for him were then added to the totals of the candidates still in the running. That process continued until one candidate had over 50%.

The Liberals thought that their supporters would automatically mark the Conservatives as their second choice, and vice versa for the Conservatives. That was one of the most significant miscalculations in BC political history. In fact, many Liberals disliked the Conservatives, and they marked the CCF or Social Credit as their second or third choices. Many Conservatives felt the same about Liberals, their second preference usually being Social Credit. The CCF was the sworn enemy of both the Liberals and the Conservatives, so many of them marked Social Credit as their second choice. The second major misjudgment of the Liberals and Conservatives was that it was the least successful candidate whose ballot was eliminated. These were, by definition, the fringe candidates, extremists, Socialists and Communists, or very unpopular candidates from the main-line parties. They were most likely to make either CCF or Social Credit their second choice.

The third major miscalculation of the Liberals and Conservatives was under-estimating the sudden rise in popularity of the Social Credit party. Social Credit had emerged in Alberta in the early 1930s, but it had never received much support in BC. However, by 1952 people were well aware that in Alberta the Social Credit party was providing competent government and had eliminated the CCF. In BC it appealed to small business, rural areas, ethnic groups who were outside the political mainstream, religious fundamentalists, people from the prairies who had moved into eastern and central BC, and small-c conservatives who felt the main parties had let them down. It had finally become well-organized, especially in the vastly over-represented rural constituencies where recent migrants from Alberta brought their enthusiasm, political experience and organizational skills.

The fourth miscalculation of the Liberals and Conservatives was in underestimating the new de facto leader of the Social Credit party. As a teenager W.A.C. Bennett had shown a keen interest in politics in his native New Brunswick. He quit high school, educated himself through correspondence courses, and grew rich in the hardware business in Alberta. In the 1930s he moved to Kelowna, built a successful chain of hardware stores, and became a millionaire. He was hard-working, religious, energetic, and popular. He was a born Conservative, but the provincial party was run by the rich urban elite which did not have much time for folks like him. He was elected as an MLA in 1949, but was never offered a Cabinet post. Twice he failed to win the Conservative leadership.

During his second campaign for the Conservative leadership Bennett travelled extensively throughout BC. There he discovered the deep discontent with the Coalition, with both main parties, and with government in general. Seeing no future in the Conservative party, he resigned in March 1951 to sit as an Independent. From the opposition benches he became a very effective critic of government mismanagement. At this time, membership in the Social Credit Party was rapidly growing in rural BC, and Bennett joined them in December. Their leader was an Albertan, but Bennett was their only MLA, and he campaigned effectively for the whole party in 1952.

When the votes were counted the first time the CCF had 31% of the popular vote, the Socreds 27%. But when they were recounted until each candidate obtained over 50%, the unthinkable had happened. The party that had entered the election as a distant fourth, that had never received more than 1.5% of the vote, that had been given no chance whatsoever, had won the most seats (19). The CCF still received more of the popular votes, 34% to the Socred's 30, but their support was more dispersed geographically which gave them one less seat. The Liberals had held on to their quarter of the vote, but that only gave them six seats. The Conservatives had massively over-estimated their own popularity, and won only four seats. It was not, however, clear who had actually won the election.

Chapter Ten
Social Credit, 1952-1972

When the counting finished six weeks after the June 1952 election, it was clear who had won the most seats, but not clear who would form the government. Harold Winch, leader of the CCF, informed the lieutenant governor that his party should govern because it had obtained more votes, had the support of the independent Socialist, and had more experienced members. W.A.C. Bennett also went to see the lieutenant governor carrying a letter of support from the Socialist MLA whom the CCF claimed was supporting them.

After considerable delay, the lieutenant governor asked Bennett to form a government. Social Credit was in power, but Bennett had no MLAs with any parliamentary experience other than himself, no lawyers, which was a prerequisite for an Attorney General, and no one with the financial experience to handle the accounts and reassure business and investors. Bennett reassured the business community by recruiting the prominent Vancouver lawyer and accountant Eisner Gunderson as Finance Minister. Robert Bonner, a cautious young Conservative lawyer and MLA, crossed the floor to become Attorney General. By-elections were arranged, and the two Vancouverites won. Social Credit was ready to govern.

Bennett's minority government introduced a budget which implemented a few of the campaign promises and increased taxes on the resource industries. But the government was not able to pass any significant legislation, and on 24 March 1953 it was defeated. The CCF leader, Harold Winch, again asked the lieutenant governor to make him premier, and again the lieutenant governor refused. Bennett asked for dissolution and an election was called.

The transferable vote system was still in effect, but this time a larger number of Liberals and Conservatives saw the Socreds as the best option. When the counting was finished, the Socred's share of the popular vote had jumped from 30 to 45% votes. It had gained nine seats and a clear majority of 28 out of 48. The CCF lost four seats for a total of 14. The Liberals lost two seats and the Conservatives lost nine. Having come to power through the vagaries of the transferable vote system, Bennett then abolished it lest he become its next victim.

Bennett had solidified his power and he would govern BC seemingly effortlessly for the next two decades. His power base was rural BC where the voters were vastly over-represented in the Assembly. Bennett then taxed urban wealth, and spent disproportionately on rural areas. He moderately increased taxes on the big resource companies which had no choice but to support the Socreds since the alternative was the CCF. He played the old game of fighting with the federal government and arguing that the electorate had to give him a strong mandate for that task. Two of his favourite themes were providing stable government and saving BC from the socialists. With these strategies almost perfectly executed by Bennett, the Socreds won seven consecutive victories between 1953 and 1969.

When Social Credit came to power the economy was still booming. Foreign investment was pouring into the resource sector, and revenue was pouring into government coffers. Bennett adopted a very simple, two-pronged approach to government. On the one hand, he plowed large amounts of money into infrastructure both to facilitate business and industry and for the use of the public. On the other, he plowed large sums into the things the people wanted and needed. There was an almost immediate increase in spending on highways, bridges, hydro-electric dams, new railway lines, schools, and hospitals.

Basically that remained Socred policy for two decades. The real debates then centered on which projects to build and how and when to build them. Bennett was a consummate politician – the launching or completion of any project provided a "photo-op" for the smiling premier as he hammered home the theme that Social Credit times were good times. Roads and schools in the interior produced far more Socred MLAs than similar expenditure in the cities, so that is where the expenditure was concentrated. Besides, in Bennett's view, the cities sopped up money from the countryside, so it was only fair for government to restore some balance by lavishing money on public works anywhere but in Victoria or the Lower Mainland.

But Bennett also acted in the interests of the entire province. He quickly solved the problem of health insurance which had plagued governments since the late 1930s. The problem was that the method of financing the program with compulsory health insurance dividends was very unpopular. So Bennett cancelled them and added one percent to the provincial sales tax. This was one of many "left-wing" measures the Socreds took, because the rich spent far more money than the poor and they therefore pay more relatively in sales taxes.

Bennett's Socred government presented itself as the great defender of private enterprise, but it carried out some of the biggest nationalizations of private companies in BC history. His small-town, anti-establishment, anti-Vancouver image was partly pure politics – Bennett spent heavily on the University of British Columbia, turned Victoria College into a University, established the new Simon Fraser University, and set up a number of community colleges. He found it valuable politically to pretend that BC was sharply divided into a centre-right portion, which SC represented, and a radical left-wing which the CCF represented. That was not an accurate description of either party, but it probably helped win elections.

One of the Socred's main promises was to provide debt-free government. To do this he changed the way government accounts were maintained. The Pacific Great Eastern Railway (PGE) had always been a drain on provincial finances. Bennett separated the two accounts, and from then on the PGE's debt was on its books rather than those of the government. Bennett did the same for the BC Power Corporation. He took the credit for massive dams and all the employment and contracts they created, but then pretended that the debt was incurred by the crown corporations and not his government.

He did the same for the highways budget, creating the Toll Bridge and Highway Authority which could charge tolls, borrow money and build roads and bridges which he would inaugurate at grand ceremonies. The government deficit rapidly dropped, debt was paid off, and Bennett declared the province debt free. And he did it in style, with a barge loaded with gasoline-soaked bonds floating off Kelowna beach, and him setting it ablaze with a burning arrow.

As the election of 1956 approached Bennett had found the winning formula. The world, Canada and BC were booming. He was adding to that with substantial spending on roads, bridges across BC's mighty rivers and a tunnel under the Fraser. Roads were important for cutting the time and cost of travel, for creating jobs, and for breaking the psychological barrier of isolation that the mountains had always imposed. Taxes on the big resource industries made him appear as a populist. In fact, those tax rates were relatively modest, and his government was making it increasingly difficult for labour to launch strikes. To silence the critics of Social Credit economic theory, he announced that every homeowner would be given a grant, a "social dividend" from the wealth of the province.

Rumours of scandals made the headlines. The most serious was the accusation that the Minister of Lands, Forests and Mines, Robert Sommers, had accepted some favours. Bennett set up an enquiry which would not report until after the election which he called for 1956. The Socred's popularity in the over-represented interior helped produce nine more seats for a total of 39 on the same percentage vote as in 1953. The CCF lost four seats for a total of ten, and the Liberals dropped to two seats. The people did not seem to regard corruption as a major issue because Mr. Sommers easily won his seat – a few years later he went to jail for accepting bribes.

In terms of timing elections, luck was with Bennett because Canada slipped into recession shortly after his re-election. His response was two-fold. First, he drastically slashed provincial spending, especially the highways budget. Second, he went looking for major projects to turn the economy around and capture people's attention or perhaps divert their attention. He thought he had found it with the Swedish company Wenner-Gren. It was to survey 1/10th of the province in the far north with a view to investing $2,000,000,000 in pulp and paper, minerals, transportation and towns. Bennett's second project to kick-start the economy was the development of the enormous hydro-electric potential of the Peace River. He announced it before any studies had been completed, and in spite of the fact that negotiations were underway with the United States to develop the power resources of the Columbia River.

The announcement of an election for 12 September 1960 was accompanied by a rash of promises for a huge road-building program, more railways in the north, more companies to invest in the Wenner-Gren project, more "social dividends" in the form of grants to homeowners, and increased expenditure on welfare. Industry was wooed with tougher anti-labour legislation and the outlawing of sympathy strikes. When ferry workers went on strike, Bennett nationalized one company and bought another, creating the BC Ferry Service. This stole more thunder from the CCF which had long advocated it. In the election the CCF put up a good fight and made some serious inroads. The Socred's lost six percent of the vote and six seats, leaving them with 32 out of 52 seats. The CCF gained six seats for 16, and the Liberals managed to hang on to four. Bennett had survived both recession and scandal.

Re-election meant getting on with the huge dam projects. The Columbia is an international river, so any agreement had to involve the Canadian and American federal governments. Unfortunately, BC and Ottawa had diametrically opposite views on the projects. Ottawa wanted Canadian power projects to serve Canadian consumers. It favoured short-term exports of power so that the electricity would be available when demand grew in Canada. Bennett wanted to develop the Peace River, and to do that he needed the rest of BC as a market for its power. He therefore wanted Columbia power exported to the United States under long-term contracts that would pay for both the Columbia and the Peace River developments. His plan also meant that the main power dams would be on the American side of the border, with holding dams on the Canadian where considerable environmental damage would occur.

The struggle reached epic proportions. To consolidate his political power, Bennett nationalized BC Electric, a privately-owned company that had provided electricity to the Lower Mainland. It was joined to the provincially-owned BC Power Corporation to form the BC Hydro and Power Authority which was now province-wide and had the added mandate of developing power on the Peace River. The public had never liked BC Electric, the shareholders got a good price, and the CCF could not object as it had long advocated the nationalization of utilities. As a private company BC Electric had paid taxes to the federal government. As a crown corporation, BC Hydro could not be taxed by Ottawa but the provincial government could devise numerous means to obtain financial and political benefits from it.

Ottawa and Victoria were still at loggerheads over the deal, but a federal election was looming. For the first time Bennett intervened in federal politics, urging people to vote Socred instead of Conservative. The federal Conservatives were reduced to a minority government which then had to accept BC's position on the Columbia River project in order to get Socred support in the House of Commons.

By then it was time for another provincial election, and Bennett sought endorsement for his grand power schemes. Just to make clear how valuable power was to every voter, he reduced the price of electricity by 11% in the Lower Mainland, and naturally, by over twice as much elsewhere. Increasing prosperity permitted the usual package of promises. Some taxes were reduced, the homeowners' "social dividend" was increased, and municipalities received more assistance. The magic formula worked again in the 1963 election, with the Socreds increasing their vote share to 41% and gaining another seat for 33 out of 52. The CCF, now called the New Democratic Party or NDP, lost five percent of the vote and two seats for a total of 14.

As in 1960, re-election meant getting on with the big dam projects, or the dam big projects as some called them. The Columbia agreement negotiated with the United States was controversial. It put the Canadian part of the river under international control but not the American side, restricted the possibility of diverting water in the future, and permanently integrated Columbian power into the American economy. Some critics argued that BC sold the power for far less than it should have. But at another impressive photo-op Bennett received a giant cheque for the first payment.

Bennett then turned his attention to creating the Bank of British Columbia. In both Alberta and BC, Social Credit had always believed that the eastern-controlled banks siphoned off deposits from the west, loaned a disproportionate amount of money to companies in the east, and received support for these practices from the federal government. Bennett's solution was to establish a local bank that would loan its money to ordinary people and small businesses. In Ottawa the Senate refused to charter the new bank, giving Bennett a good excuse to ask the people for a new mandate to stand up for their interests.

The province was booming, and numerous newspapers and magazines hailed the premier as a man of vision, the champion of free enterprise, full employment, prosperity, and good times. The W.A.C.Bennett Dam was inaugurated on the Peace River in 1967, creating the largest man-made lake in the world. It was time for another election. The Socreds gained five percent more of the popular vote (45%), but no additional seats. The NDP's vote went from 28 to 34%, giving it only two more seats. With five successful elections to his credit, Bennett was now the longest serving head of government at any level in North America.

Again re-election meant more of the same. Bennett opened a number of dams on the Peace and Columbia Rivers. But their completion increased unemployment just as the economy was sliding into recession. The dams were supposed to provide BC with low-cost power, but they cost more than estimated, and BC Hydro had to increase the price of electricity. Ottawa had finally approved the charter for the Bank of British Columbia, but few people wanted to invest in it, and it was eventually taken over by a foreign bank.

Scandals had always been a backdrop to BC politics, and now they became more serious. It seemed that the two sons of Highway Minister Phil Gaglardi had an uncanny knowledge of where roads were going to be built, resulting in high profits on investments in real estate along those roads. Gaglardi, known as "Flying Phil" because of his reputation for speeding, was forced to resign. He had been a key Cabinet Minister. Robert Bonner, the Conservative who had brought stability to Bennett's first administration as Attorney General and been a pillar in it ever since, decided to retire from politics. The loss of five by-elections suggested that the party was in serious decline.

Bennett was perhaps at his best when facing a crisis. He called an election for 27 August 1969, sustaining the pattern of elections every three years. The efficacy of fighting Ottawa during provincial elections had been proven for almost a century, so he made an issue of whether offshore resources were federal or provincial. Like Premier Pattullo he proposed to annex the Yukon as well as the western Northwest Territories. He announced new spending, reduced ferry fares, put more restrictions on labour unions, and blamed the increasing number of strikes on the NDP. The magic formula worked even better, as the Socred's vote increased to 47%, the highest ever. That gave Bennett five more seats for a total of 38. The NDP's support held steady but they lost four seats for a total of 16.

Bennett and his policies had been vindicated by the people for the sixth consecutive time, and he went back to work building his beloved province. But his luck was definitely running out. The completion of most of the huge public works projects meant those workers were unemployed, and contracts for cement, machinery and supplies dried up. To deal with high costs, companies were acquiring more labour-saving machinery which added to labour discontent. Unemployment increased to nearly 10%. There were no major public works to take up the slack, and no money for them either. Canada was experiencing very high inflation, and strikes increased as workers fought to maintain their standard of living.

The BC of 1970 was a very different province from that of 1950. Its population had almost doubled again, from 1,165,000 to 2,185,000. The vast majority lived in cities and much of that was immigrant. The Socred's natural base of white, rural Protestants was a shrinking portion of the new BC. Over the years the Socreds had gradually lost its populist image as it became clear that big business was fully behind the party and that the party looked after big business. At the age of seventy, Bennett had been in politics for 30 years, 20 as premier. He seemed to lose direction and energy, and grew aloof from the public. His government also began to drift. One example was needlessly picking fights with the teacher's union – in the 1950s, groups like teachers were part of Social Credit's vote bank. The government had looked after them, but now it was driving them into the welcome arms of the NDP, and it had a new leader. An era was coming to a close, and Bennett seemed to sense it.

Chapter Eleven

New Democrats and New Social Creditors, 1972-1985

As the 1970s dawned it became increasingly clear that Bennett and his government had lost both their magical touch and run out of luck. As unemployment increased the government argued that the problem was welfare fraud, which infuriated people without addressing the issue. The government reacted to growing discontent in major unions like teachers and welfare workers with restrictive measures instead of compromises. Bennett's accounting practices drew criticism, especially loaning money from pension funds to crown corporations at preferred rates which basically meant that civil servants were subsidizing government-owned companies.

The old formula of saving the province from the union bosses had paid political dividends when the unions in question were concentrated in a few mining towns. But health and education workers lived in every town and city, looked after their neighbours and taught their children. Their union leaders could not be branded as privileged, dictatorial or Communist. The old gimmick of fighting with Ottawa was wearing thin. Ottawa was moving to the left, and many in BC supported federal policies such as restrictions on foreign investment. In contrast, Bennett was seen by many as being too willing to make deals to attract foreign investment and not sufficiently concerned with the long-term interests of the province.

There was discontent across Canada in the early 1970s, and BC had its share. Bennett's old argument – that investment in hydro-electric dams was good for everyone – was hard to defend when electricity bills were going up. The government paid scant attention to the growing public awareness of environmental damage. Reforestation lagged far behind the rate at which forests were being cut down. Bennett announced new mega projects. One was for giant mines that delivered an endless supply of coal to the artificial island port of Roberts Bank for delivery to Japan. But these heavily-automated operations produced few jobs, damaged the environment, and led to criticism that the province had given away too much for too little. The mood of the people was sour, and they complained about rising taxes and car insurance rates and falling relative incomes.

To add to Bennett's woes, the NDP had a new and effective leader in David Barrett. Like Bennett, he was outspoken, decisive, and flamboyant. But he was also a generation younger, and was a populist from a poor working-class background in Vancouver. He was smart, funny, vigorous, a good speaker, and a good organizer. As a social worker he had seen the rougher side of life while working with prisoners. First elected in 1960, he did not join the inner circle of the CCF-NDP which had failed to gain more than 33% of the public's support. In 1970 he won by acclamation his second bid to lead the party. He immediately broadened the party's platform and reached out to the party membership and other groups like farmers, small businessmen, civil servants, teachers and geographic regions the Socreds had neglected.

The election of 1972 ended the first Social Credit experiment. Its share of the popular vote plunged from an all-time high of 47 to 31%. Now the distortion in distribution worked against it, cutting its seat total from 38 to ten. The NDP increased its share of the vote from 34 to 40%, and that more than tripled its seats from 12 to 38. The Liberals continued to lose votes but held onto their five seats, and the Conservatives jumped to 13% of the popular vote but won only two seats. The system of unfair distribution, single constituencies and first-past-the post counting that had been used to keep the CCF-NDP out of office for forty years had now worked to its advantage. And they were determined to seize the opportunity that holding power finally presented.

The NDP set out to implement the policies it had advocated since the Depression. There were immediate increases to pensions, education, health and daycare. Many of the restrictions Bennett had placed on labour unions were removed, the labour code was updated, and the minimum wage was increased by one-third. A Pharmacare program was instituted for seniors. Racial discrimination was banned in employment and housing. BC soon had the most effective consumer's protection legislation in Canada. Barrett froze rents to deal with one of the most serious effects of inflation. The Assembly was made more meaningful, sessions longer, and debates properly recorded.

New legislation flowed through the Assembly at ten times the rate as under the previous government. Car insurance companies had long been accused of excess billing so a government monopoly was created to guarantee fair fees. Complaints had grown about urban sprawl eating up the rustic rural lands of the Fraser delta – Barrett made it illegal to sell agricultural land for urban development. When the Ocean Falls pulp and paper plant was about to close, the provincial government took it over to preserve the jobs. The BC Petroleum Corporation was established to assist in the development of that resource.

While many people benefited from these policies, many were opposed, including business, industry, land developers, and those with investment in real estate. The NDP believed that the merits of its policies would be self-evident, when more explanation and publicity could have broadened the appeal of those policies. Barrett believed that cooperation with Ottawa was more profitable than squabbling, so he made peace on that front. And the economy cooperated, with boom years from 1971 to 1973.

Then the NDP's fortunes changed suddenly for the worse. The economy slowed just as the bills were coming in for the dramatic increases in social spending and the new programs. The province's finances quickly descended into serious deficit, providing ammunition for the party's critics and enemies. BC Hydro raised the price of electricity, and it was owned by the government which had criticized privately-owned car insurance companies for raising their premiums.

It was argued that the NDP's new government-owned monopoly had raised car insurance premiums to give its workers inflated wage increases. A rash of strikes broke out as workers tried to keep pace with inflation, and the NDP found itself in the unenviable position of opposing legitimate strikes in order to keep vital services running. That was a problem of its own making, because in the first flush of its long-awaited victory it had given the right to strike to public servants. Now it had to tell them they could not use it.

Barrett and the NDP had delivered on the long-postponed platform of the CCF, and their followers were delighted with the quick transformation of the province. But they had made serious political miscalculations concerning the 60% of the population that had voted for other parties in 1972. Many of the NDP's reforms created opposition, so the faster they introduced them the bigger, more determined and more united that opposition became. Small increases in the minimum wage could have been absorbed; a sudden, one-third increase brought hardship to many businesses. In these circumstances Barrett decided to call an election. It was three years into the NDP's mandate, two years before an election was due, and a week before redistribution would have given the party more seats. It was a period when problems were mounting and the benefits of the many good initiatives of the government had not yet taken effect, had not been well publicized, or were not yet recognized by many voters.

Wacky Bennett had retired after his defeat in 1972 campaign. He had so dominated the party that there were no first-class lieutenants ready to replace him. The party then turned to his son, William, who became known as "Miniwac". He lacked some of his father's political talents, but he was as young as Barrett and was untainted with scandal or failure. He was well aware that Social Credit had grown out of touch, and that many of Barrett's initiatives were both good and long overdue. It seemed that Barrett's mistake was to have gone too far, too fast, and to have mismanaged the province's finances, not to have done the wrong things. Bennett's basic plan, therefore, was to promise to continue Barrett's policies, but to do so in a businesslike manner. He promised to maintain and improve policies like Pharmacare, protect jobs in the crown corporations, and cut government spending and taxes. That was a message the Liberals and Conservatives were eager to hear.

When the votes were counted, the NDP had maintained its 1972 peak vote, proving that its followers were well satisfied with its performance in power. But ten percent of the voters had abandoned the Liberals and another eight had abandoned the Conservatives. Those voters were determined to defeat the NDP, and the Socred vote jumped from 30 to 49%, a peak Wacky Bennett had never achieved. The NDP went from 38 seats to 18; the Socreds from 10 to 35. BC's first experience with NDP government had ended in just three years

Bill Bennett proved to be almost as decisive and pragmatic as his father, easily winning re-election in 1979. He did not slash the size of the civil service as his supporters might have wanted and his critics certainly feared, and that ensured peace within the civil service. He carried on with some of the reformist thrust of the NDP, appointing an ombudsman to listen to the complaints of citizens and perhaps encourage government to respond. He appointed an auditor-general, a measure that suggested that he was abandoning the questionable book-keeping practices his father had used. He put an immediate free-enterprise stamp on his regime by selling off the government-owned pulp and paper company, Canadian Cellulose. And he rationalized the structure of crown corporations by bringing them together under a single administration called the British Columbia Resources Industry Corporation, or BCRIC.

Because it was a government-owned crown corporation, every citizen of the province theoretically owned a share of BCRIC. But in a move typical of Social Creditors, the government issued every citizen with five shares in BCRIC. That gave them a concrete, de facto proof of ownership, and they could sell or trade those shares on the stock exchange. In 1979 Bennett called an election on the old free-enterprise vs. socialism theme that had worked so well for Social Credit and the Coalition before it. The choice, he argued, was between NDP-style state-ownership or individual ownership. It was, of course, a false choice since in both scenarios the government owned the crown corporations and the government ultimately belonged to the people.

The NDP had remained a strong alternative under Barrett, and the people saw the election of 1979 as a clear fight between two visions of the province and two systems for running it. Social Credit lost one percentage point of the popular vote which gave it a slimmer majority of 31. The NDP picked up seven percentage points for an all-time high of 46% and a gain of eight seats for 26. The Liberal vote collapsed and they were shut out of the Assembly for the first time since 1903. Now both the province and the Assembly were sharply and evenly divided, and both parties would begin the eighties with strong leaders, experienced MLAs, determined supporters and strong organizations.

Bennett then revived his father's economic and political strategy of development through mega-projects. The Coquihalla Highway connected

Vancouver with Kelowna over the southern part of the province, cutting hours off the trip. The old dreams for major development in the Peace River country were revisited with plans to develop the extensive coal reserves. Though not the direct result of Bennett's policies, Vancouver figured prominently in the New Rome, with Expo 86, urban renewal, waterfront development, and with Skytrain and Light-Rail Transit to whisk the growing suburban population to and from the city centre. An election in 1983 confirmed Bill Bennett's political acumen as the Socreds hit another all-time high in popular vote – 50% - which brought it back to a solid majority of 35. The NDP held 45% of the vote but lost four seats. This time both Liberals and Conservatives were crushed, as more and more people saw politics as a clash of left and right.

The British Columbia of the mid-1980s was a land of sharp paradoxes reflective perhaps of the rugged contrasts of its geography. It was bitterly divided politically, between business and labour, between rich and poor. As the new skyscrapers changed the face of western Vancouver, mere blocks away the centre was deteriorating into a slum infamous for its drug culture. An economic recession was met by a government program of massive restraint, which in turn galvanized those affected into a resistance movement known as "Solidarity". A strong, determined and experienced opposition strenuously resisted in the Assembly, and tempers flared as the government used its majority and all-night sittings to impose its program.

Polarization increased as people saw the issues as ideological, political, economic and personal, particularly if they were among the thousands of civil servants being dismissed. Massive strikes began, especially amongst aggrieved groups like the teachers. The strikes were met with further resistance by the government, more restrictions on labour, and the dismissal of school boards that opposed the new policies.

While these political issues dominated the headlines, a profound change was underway in the rapid growth of Asian economies, the even more rapid growth of trade and investment across the Pacific, and the increasing economic integration of the Pacific region. Asia had become the main source of immigration to Canada, and BC was one of the main destinations. These developments produced profound changes in the economy, the population, the cities and the culture. From being one of the most isolated frontiers in the world in the eighteenth century, BC was beginning to enjoy the benefits of centrality in the global economy of the twenty-first century.

As the 1980s unfolded, the BC economy remained strong and wage rates were the highest in Canada. The people bragged of the best standard of living, the best life style, the best climate, a flowering of the arts, first-class facilities for everything from sports to concerts to conventions, and an attitude that BC politics had always been rather bizarre anyway. Canadians outside BC continued to view the land beyond the Rockies, the "West beyond the West", as both distant and odd, a bit like the rest of Canada, but not quite part of it. That, too, was how its citizens saw it. And Canadians from east of the Rockies continued to migrate to BC in large numbers as they had for a century, drawn to its cities, its river valleys, its climate and its mountains. In the coming decades, BC's share of Canada's wealth and population would continue to increase. Its self-confidence and optimism would see it through more downturns in the economy, and it would occupy a place of growing importance in the nation's affairs.

Suggestions for Further Reading

British Columbia has been well served by its historians. The old standard text *British Columbia: A History* was written by Margaret Ormsby, Head of the Department of History at the University of British Columbia (Vancouver, 1958). A more up-to-date and excellent text is *The West beyond the West: a History of British Columbia* by Dr. Jean Barman (Toronto, 1991). Dr. Patricia Roy and Dr. John Herd Thompson have contributed *British Columbia: Land of Promise* to the Illustrated History of Canada series (Don Mills, 2005). A wonderfully-written book is George Woodcock's *British Columbia* (Vancouver, 1990), and his *A Picture History of British Columbia* (Edmonton, 1980) is excellent. Terry Reksten has also produced *An Illustrated History of British Columbia* (Vancouver, 2001).

Martin Robin wrote a definitive history of the interplay of politics, economics and business in *The Rush For Spoils: The Company Province* (Toronto, 1972) and *Pillars of Profit: The Company Province* (Toronto, 1973). In addition to a wealth of information and analysis, these books prove that serious history can be very entertaining. There is a great collection of essays on various aspects of BC's history in *The Pacific Province,* edited by Hugh Johnston (Vancouver, 1966). Any province is the sum of its parts, and one example of regional history is *They Call It The Cariboo* by Robin Skelton (Victoria, 1980). Before the age of computers historians often wrote wonderful prose that is a joy to read even if the benefits of modern research are lacking. An example is *British Columbia: The Making of a Province* by F.W. Howay (Toronto, 1928). Finally, a somewhat humorous account is *Bowering's BC: A Swashbucking History* by George Bowering (Toronto, 1996).

Index

Agriculture, 8,13,24,26
Alaska, 2,4,7,14,28,48 49
Alberta, 1,2,7,16,20,41,45,50,52
Alcan, 50
America, Americans, United States, 4,5,7,8,10,11,12,14,20,28,31,32,38, 48,56-57
Amor de Cosmos, 13, 23
Anglicans, 8,12,31
Anscomb, Herbert, 51
Arctic Ocean, 1,2,12
Asia, Asians, 1,1-32, 0, 0
Athapaskan, 2
Atlantic Ocean, 4

Bank of British Columbia, 57,8
Barkerville, 11
Barrett, David, 60-63
Beaven, Robert, 23, 4
The Beaver, 8
Bella Coola River, 2,5
Bering Strait, 1
Bering, Vitrus, 4
Better terms, 19,33,42
BC Electric, 56
BC Ferry Service, 56
BC Hydro, 56
BC Petroleum Corporation, 61
BC Power Corporation, 55
BC Resource Industry Corporation (BCRIC), 63
Bennett, W.A.C., 52-60, 62, 63
Bennett, William, 62-64
Boer War, 31

Bonner, Robert, 53, 58
Bow River, 20
Bowser, William, 37,42
Brewster, Harlan, 37,38
The British Colonist, 13
The British Columbian, 14
British North America, 7,9,13
Burrard Inlet, 18,20,22
Bute Inlet, 18

Calgary, 44
California, 8,10,20
Canadian Cellulose, 63
Canadian National Railway (CNR), 37,38
Canadian Northern Railway, 34-5,37
Canadian Pacific Railway (CPR), 22-22,24,25,31,34,42
Cape Horn, 4,14
Cariboo Region, Trail, 2,11,18,21
Lord Carnarvon, 19
Cartier, George Etienne, 15
Castlegar, 33
Catholics, 31
Central Canada, 29,41,42
Chilcotin Natives, Plateau, 2,18
Chile, 36
China, Chinese, 4,5,10,17,20-22,31-32,38,50
Coalition, The, 50-53,48,63
Coastal Mountains, 1
Columbia River, 1,2,4,5,7,8,12,56-58
Cominco, 26
Communism, 43

Confederation, 10,13-17,31,
Conscription, 39
Conservative Party (federal),
19,30,45,57
Conservative Party (provincial) 30-
31,33,35,37,38,41,41,42,44,46,47,48,
51,52,53,61,62
Co-operative Commonwealth Federa-
tion (CCF), 44-5,46,47,48,50,51,52,.
53,55,56,57
Coquihalla Highway, 63
Cook, James, 4
Craigellachie, 22
Cree, 2
Crowsnest Pass, 20,25,
Currie, Arthur, 36

Davie, Theodore, 23
Dawson Creek, 40,49
Depression, The, 40,43-47,48
Dominion Coal Company, 35
Douglas James, 6-13,27
Doukhobors, 33
Lord Dufferin, 19-20
Dunsmuir, Robert, 25,26,27

East India, East Indians, see India
Economic policy, 24-26
Edmonton, 20,35
Elections, 1903: 31, 1906: 33; 1909:
35, 1912: 35, 1916: 37, 1920: 40,
1924: 41, 1933:   44-5, 1937:
46, 1848: 48, 1945: 50, 1949: 51,
1952: 51-3, 1953: 53, 1956: 55, 1960:
56, 1963: 57, 1967: 57, 1969: 58,
1972: 61, 1975: 62-3, 1979: 63
Elliott, Andrew Charles, 23
Empress Hotel, 31
England, English, Great Britain,
4,5,6,8-14, 18, 20,26,28,29,31-

3,36,40,48
Esquimalt, 7,8,15,18,19,20,22,25,36
Europe, Europeans, 5,6,10,29,32-33

Fernie,26
Finlay, W.C.,38
Fishing, 24-6
Forestry, 8,13,24-6,41,50
Fort Astoria, 5
Fort McLeod, 5
Fort Vancouver, 7,8
Fraser River, 1,2,5,8,10,11,12,16,18,
20,26,46,61
Fraser, Simon, 5
Fur trade, 5,6-9

Gaglardi, Phil, 58
Gastown, 22
General Post Office, 47
Georgia Strait, 18
Germany, Germans, 32,33,36
Gold rush, 10-11,27,31.33
Golden, 20,24
Goodwin, Albert, 39
Grand Forks, 33
Grand Trunk Pacific, 35
Granville, 22
Gray, Robert, 4
Greece, 50
Gulf of Mexico, 1
Gundersn, Eisner, 53

Haida peoles, 2
Harrison Lake, 11
Hart, John, 48,50
Hawaii, 8,32,48
Hernandez, Juan Josef Perez, 4
Hindus, 32
Hong Kong, 2448
Hope, 1,2,8

Hotel Georgia, 47
Howse Pass, 5
Hudson's Bay Company (HBC), 5,6-10,12,13

Immigration, 23,31-2,50
India, 17,21,32,50
Italy, Italians, 32,33,50

Japan, Japanese,17,21,26,32,38, 48-9,50
Jasper, 20
Jews, 10,33
Johnson, Byron, 51

Kamloops, 20,24,34
Kelowna, 54,5564
Keynesian economics, 4
Kicking Horse Pass, 20
Kimberley, 26
King, Mackenzie, 37
Kitimat, 50
Klondike, 27,28
Kootenaay peoles, region, 2,5,7,25,26,35
Kwalkiutl peoples, 2

Labour, 40
Lake Ontario, 9
Lake Superior, 21
Lakehead, 41
Legislative Assembly, 9,12,13,14,18,19,20,21,23-4,31,35,61
Legislative Council, 12, 13
Liberal Party (federal), 19,30,45,47
Liberal Party (provincial), 30,31,33,35,37,38,40,41,42,44,46,47,48,51,52,53,55,56,61,62
Lillooet, 2,11
London, 1,5,12,14,20,24,35,50

Lower Mainland, 1,2,29
Lusitania, 35
Lytton, 2

McBride, Richard, 29-31
McCreight, John Foster, 17,23
McGill University, 35
McInnis, 24
Mackenzie, Alexander, 5,19
McLean, 42
Macdonald, John A., 14,15,19,20
McRae, A.D., 41
Manitoba, 13,14,15,16,31,41
Martin, Joseph, 24,30
Maritime Provinces, 43
Metis, 6,9
Methodists, 31
Mexico, 4,5
Mining, 8,10-3,24-6,41
Monashee Mountains, 1
Montreal 4,7,14
Musgrave, Anthony, 14-5

Nanaimo, 8,18,19,20,22,25,26
Natives, 1-11, 13, 17, 27, 32-3, 50
Nelson, 26
New Brunswick, 14,15
New Caledonia, 5,6,12
New Democratic Party (NDP), 57,58,61,3,64
New Westminster, 12,13,14,46
New York, 43
Nootka peoples, 2,3
Nootka Sound, 4
North America, 1,4,5,14,24
Northwest Passage, 4
Northwest Territories, 58
North West Company (NWC) 5,7
Nova Scotia, 14,15

Ocean Falls Company, 61
Okanagan, 2,7,25,26
Oliver, John, 39-42
On-to-Ottawa Trek, 46
Onderdonk, Andrew, 21,22
Ontario, 14,31,36,41
Oregon, 7

Pacific Grand Eastern Railway (PGE), 35,37,38,40,46,49,55
Pacific Ocean, 2,4,5,7,8,14,20,24,64
Parsnip River, 5
Pattullo, Duff, 44-48, 58
Peace River, region, 1,2,5,12,20,22,40, 46,49,56-8,64
Pearl Harbour, 48
People's Prohibition Party, 38
Pharmacare, 61
Port Moody, 22
Polk, James, 7-8
Portugal, 50
Potlatches, 3,6
Presbyterians, 31
Prince George, 2,35
Prince Rupert, 2,8,28,35,49
Prior, E.G., 30
Progressive Party, 41
Prohibition, 35,37,38,40
Purcell Mountains, 1

Quadra, Juan Francisco, 4
Quebec, 14
Queen Charotte Islands, 1,2 4
Quesnel, 40

Racial discrimination, 21-2,31-3,48-50,61
Red River, 15
Regina, 46
Representative government, 17

Responsible government, 13,17,18,23,40
Revelstoke, 20,21,22,24
Roberts Bank, 60
Robson, John, 14,23
Rocky Mountains, Rockies, 1,2,5,7,8,12,18,20,21,65
Rogers, A.B., 20
Roosevelt, Franklin, 45
Rossland, 26
Rowell-Sirois Report, 47
Royal Engineers, 11,12
Royal Navy, 7
Rupert's Land, 12,14
Russia, Russians, 4,6,714

Salish people, 2,3
San Francisco, 10,15
Saskatchewan, 5,16,17
Scandinavians, 32,33
Scots, Scottish, 5
Seattle, 28,36
Selkirk Mountains, 1
Semlin, Charles, 24
Siberia, 1
Sikhs, 32
Simon Fraser University, 54
Simpson, George, 7
Singapore, 48
Skeena Mountains, 1
Slave peoples, 2
Slavs, 33
Smith, Bill, 13
Solidarity, 64
Spain, Spanish, 4
Squamish, 40
Social Credit Party (Socreds), 45, 52-64
Socialists, 33, 35,40,41,45,52
Sommers, Robert, 55

South Africa, 29
Stanley Park, 24
Statute of Westminster, 48
Strait of Georgia, 1
Strikes, 38-9, 41, 62
Supreme Court, 21

Temperance League, 38
Thompson, David, 5
Thompson River, 2,20
Tlingit people, 2
Toll Bridge and Highway Authority, 55
Tolmie, Simon Fraser, 42,44
Trail, 20,26
Tsimshian people, 2
Trutch, Joseph, 17,23,24
Turner, John, 24

United States, see America
University of British Columbia, 59
University of Victoria, 54

Vancouver, 1,2,7,22,24,28,29,32,34,
35,37,40,41,42,43,44,47,64
Vancouver Art Gallery, 47
Vancouver, George, 4
Vancouver Island, 1,2,4,7,8,10,11,12,
12,18,22,26,27
Veregin, Peter, 33
Victoria, 7,8,10,13,15,18,20,24,28,
31,42
Victoria, Queen, 12

Walkem, George, 19, 23
Washington State, 8
Watson Lake, 49
Wenner-Gren, 55, 56
West Road River, 5
Winch, Harold, 53
Winnipeg General Strike, 39

Woman's Suffrage, 35,37,38
World War I, 29,31,35-9,43,48,50
World War II, 45-48

Yale, 11,20, 22,29
Yellowhead Pass, 20,34
Yukon, 1,2,46-749,58